Working for Yourself

Running a business, starting a company or being self-employed

Roger Mason

First published in paperback 2014

Thorogood Publishing Ltd
10-12 Rivington Street
London EC2A 3DU
Telephone: 020 7749 4748
Fax: 020 7729 6110

Email: info@thorogoodpublishing.co.uk
Web: www.thorogoodpublishing.co.uk

A CIP catalogue record for this book is available from the
British Library.

ISBN 1 85418827 5

978 185418827 4

Preface

I have written quite a few books and most of them have been on topics suggested to me by the publisher. Just a few have been proposed
by me to the publisher and this comes into that category. I suggested
it because I can see a big need for it and because I believe that I am
well qualified to write it. Thorogood quickly saw it too and I am grate-
ful to them for enthusiastically adopting my proposal.

The need for this book is high because many people are currently
setting up their own business or thinking of doing so. Some of them
are doing it because they want the freedom and lifestyle that comes
with working for yourself. Their reasons are positive and they want to
do it regardless of the employment alternatives. Many others are
doing so because they have lost their jobs or fear that they soon will.
At the time of writing the economic climate is awful and we are reading almost daily of company closures and redundancies. Alternative
career opportunities are often few and far between, and in some
cases virtually non-existent. Your own business is almost always an
option, and it is one that a lot of people are taking.

If you are considering setting up your own business, you certainly
need information and some hard facts. You will find these in this
book, Chapter 10 on dealing with tax being an example. You will
probably also appreciate an insight into useful character traits and the

attributes necessary for success, as well as such things as the advantages and disadvantages of working from home. These are there too and I hope that you think that a useful balance has been struck.

Both my wife and I have experience with our own businesses and I hope that this is reflected in the book. I am a Chartered Certified Accountant and a Chartered Secretary, and I was employed for many years, generally happily, as a finance director and company secretary. During each of the last few of these years, and in my own time, I prepared and presented a few seminars. I also wrote a few books. Although I was paid it was done mainly because I enjoyed doing it, but I had in my mind that it could, if necessary, be a full-time business. In fact I enjoyed it so much that I began to consider choosing to go down this route.

My last couple of years as a finance director were not happy and I made preparations to be self-employed as a seminar presenter and writer on a full-time basis. This was prudent because the owner of the business eventually decided that we should part company, which he did in a very fair way. He made a bad mistake as subsequent events showed, but of course I would say that. Looking back it was one of the best things that ever happened to me. For the last fourteen years I have been happily and successfully self-employed as a seminar presenter, writer and consultant, my special subjects being company law and finance.

My wife has had a number of businesses and for the last eight years she has been self-employed as a civil funeral celebrant. Her advice in writing this book has been extremely helpful. Hopefully you will think that our record helps make this a practical book. We have actually done it. Most of the chapters end with a short note relating to our practical experiences in the areas covered by the chapter.

Having your own business may or may not be technically the same thing as being self-employed. It depends on the legal form of your business and how it is structured. In practical terms though, in most circumstances, they are likely to mean much the same. Both are used extensively in this book and in many areas they are virtually inter-changeable.

It just remains for me to thank my friend Paul Murphy for his help with the Social Networking section of Chapter 7 and to hope that you find the book useful, interesting and enjoyable. If you do take the plunge and start your own business, you have my very best wishes for success.

Table of Contents

Chapter 3

Some fundamental early decisions 39

Chapter 4

Available advice and information........................55

Chapter 5

The business plan and break-even calculation.............65

Chapter 6

Funding the business... 89

Chapter 7

Finding your customers......................................101

Chapter 10

Chapter 1

Is Self-employment right for you?

This chapter tries to help you answer the all-important question posed in its title. Topics covered are:

- The advantages and disadvantages of self-employment
- Reasons for choosing self-employment
- Helpful character traits and attributes
- Can you afford to take the risk?
- The chances of success
- Editorial comment
- Our personal experiences

The advantages and disadvantages of self-employment

Assuming that you have not yet made a commitment to self-employment and perhaps even if you have, it is a good idea to make a comparison between employment and self-employment, and to think through the advantages and disadvantages of moving from one to the other. You have probably done this already but this section of the chapter should help if you have not. Even if you have done the exercise it is worth studying what follows as it may give you fresh perspectives.

It is both inevitable and desirable that your assessment of the advantages and disadvantages of self-employment is very personal to you. You may or may not agree with the considerations that follow and you will certainly have views about the order in which they should be ranked. You can and should add further ones that occur to you. You might disagree with what follows and with the views of other people, and you might even consider some of the so-called advantages to be disadvantages and vice versa. Having said all that and in no particular order, the following are some of the advantages and disadvantages of moving from employment to self-employment.

Advantages of self-employment

- The chance to achieve your full potential
- The chance to achieve a sense of satisfaction in your work
- The chance to do what you enjoy doing
- The freedom to work in the way that suits you best
- The possibility of working in a family-friendly way
- You cannot be sacked or made redundant
- The possibility of earning a lot of money
- The absence of in-house bureaucracy
- The possibility of eliminating or reducing commuting

- The knowledge that financial rewards will be directly linked to your skill and effort
- The possibility of tax advantages
- You do not have to take orders from people that you do not like or respect
- The possibility of having a lot of fun

Disadvantages of self-employment

- The business might fail and you could lose money, perhaps a lot of money
- You might miss the support given by specialists in your employer
- You might miss the friendship of colleagues
- It will be the end of safe, secure, regular salary payments
- It will be the end of fringe benefits
- You must totally fund your pension
- The fear of the unknown. You could be operating out of your comfort zone
- The demands of self-employment might stretch you too far
- You might have to work harder and longer than you want to
- You will have to find your own customers
- It might take over your life
- It might be difficult to maintain a good balance between work, your family and the rest of your life
- There is no sick pay

Reasons for choosing self-employment

There are many reasons for choosing self-employment and most of them have at least some merit. Eight common ones follow and may be among the ones that are relevant to you. Whatever your reasons for considering the life-changing step of self-employment if you are, they should at least provide food for thought.

A good business idea

I watch the television programme Dragons' Den and see people with business ideas pitch for an investment. Almost without exception the pitch features an invention, a new idea or a novel way of doing business. This is of course because it makes good television. Some of the ideas are silly and cynically put in just to entertain us, even if it embarrasses their proponents. Some are serious prospects and a very few are sensational. If you have an invention or a novel idea, congratulations. You may do very well, though the failure rate is high.

You will not see on Dragons' Den someone who wants to open a hairdressing salon or do any of the thousands of things that are being done already. This is because these proposals would not make good television and the viewers would switch off, but of course something along these lines suits numerous people who set up their own businesses. If your locality has room for a good hairdressing salon and if you have a good business plan to provide one, this could be the right business for you. It does not have to be exciting. It does though have to be well thought out, realistic and right for you.

The associated freedom

It is known that a major factor in low stress levels, job satisfaction and happiness is a large amount of freedom to make decisions and organise one's own job. If this is true for employees and it is, it must be a big consideration for the self-employed too. You can work long hours or short hours, you can work hard or not work hard, you can choose which jobs to accept and which jobs not to accept. You can decide that you do not like someone and will not deal with them. You can make these decisions and many others too. Of course some employees have the freedom to make decisions but many do not, and virtually none have as much freedom as the self-employed. It should not escape your notice that decisions have consequences, some of them perhaps unseen and some of them perhaps unpleasant.

Family or other commitments

Inflexible working hours and the other demands of employment make life difficult for many. This applies to a wide range of people but working mothers are an obvious example. They may have to juggle the demands of work with their responsibilities in school holidays, and also during the sickness of their children and when the school is closed because of such things as bad weather. It is usually not easy, and to add insult to injury childcare is often very expensive. In fact it can take a significant part of the net earnings from employment. Some employers are more sympathetic and family-friendly than others and some employers are more able to help than others, but it is a very common problem.

Self-employment may be the answer. A job that can be done from home or a job that can be done at a time that suits you can save a lot of worry. It may also save a lot of expense on such things as child-care. Of course the job must be done even if you are self-employed – especially if you are self-employed, but the flexibility can be very attractive.

Threatened or actual dismissal or redundancy

There is a lot of it about, or at least there is at the time of writing. Hundreds of thousands (or even more) are facing the prospect or the reality of losing their jobs. What is more there are not many other jobs about, again at the time of writing. Many of those affected and their families feel angry and frustrated and they think, probably with good reason, that what is happening to them is not their fault. The job security that many of our parents and grandparents took for granted is a thing of the past.

For almost all of these people self-employment can be a serious option. Some professionals (such as accountants, architects and IT specialists) have skills that can readily be turned to good use, but self-employment is a possibility for almost all. It should provide a source of income and the satisfaction of knowing that you will not be dismissed or made redundant again. Admittedly your business could fail, but the future would be in your own hands.

Tax advantages

As we all know, there is very little scope for employees to legitimately reduce the tax and national insurance that they pay on their salaries and benefits, though of course some do so by illegal means. Tax and national insurance is deducted at source under the PAYE system.

There is however some scope for the self-employed to legitimately minimise the amount taken by Her Majesty's Government. It is a big subject and there are tax advantages and disadvantages to self-employment, but it is probably correct to say that on balance it is better to be self-employed. These advantages are explored in Chapter 10.

The possibility of making a lot of money

There is a ceiling on the earnings of employees. For a few it is a high ceiling and for a very few it may be an extremely high ceiling. For a significant number it is enough to fund a prosperous and enjoyable lifestyle, but for many others the realistic ceiling to their potential earnings is disappointing. For the owners of a business the sky is the limit, though only a few will achieve very considerable wealth. Most of them do not aspire to do so, perhaps because they know that it is not a realistic prospect for them and perhaps because they are not willing to take the necessary risks and make the necessary sacrifices. It may be because they and their families will be happy with a merely comfortable existence.

On the other hand just a few of the people who opt for self-employment will become seriously rich and many more will become moderately rich. To do this it is necessary for them to own a business, not just to get paid for working for a business. To take just two obvious examples, Sir Philip Green and Sir Richard Branson did not make their hundreds of millions (or more) by banking a salary. The wealth of the owners of a few businesses greatly exceeds the wealth of even the most highly paid directors and executives.

Passion for a hobby

Everyone should have a hobby. Many of us do and many of us enjoy the time that we spend on it more than the time that we spend earning our living. Some of us could combine the two and earn our living by pursuing our hobby. The possibilities are endless. A stamp collector could become a stamp dealer and a person who enjoys gardening could do it professionally.

Knowledge and love of the business are likely to contribute to the success of the venture, but there is a trap that must be avoided. This is to forget that it must be a business first and a hobby second. Some people put it the other way round and the consequences can be painful.

Difficulty in getting anything else

There is much that is positive in this chapter and in this book, but this sounds a horribly negative reason for choosing self-employment. Perhaps it is, but it is only being realistic to recognise that some people find it extremely difficult or virtually impossible to find a job as an employee. This may be for a number of reasons but older workers who have lost their jobs often face great problems. This is often very unfair and it is short-sighted of employers. In many cases discrimination is against the law, but it still happens. Some form of self-employment is almost always an option and making a success of it will be a wonderful morale booster. You might even see it as a form of revenge on the silly people who would not give you a job.

A final reason for self-employment is that it may be a factor contributing to a happy and long semi-retirement. Some years ago a study was conducted with the aim of discovering groups of people who lived the longest. The following distinct groups were identified:

- The self-employed

- Those with an absorbing hobby or interest

- The congenitally lazy

It was believed that the self-employed were on the list because they did not have to retire, because they enjoyed their job and their life, and because they could not afford the time off to be ill. Sudden and complete retirement can be devastating, especially for men. It is sometimes not much fun for their wives either. This is because they sometimes fill part of their time by trying to manage their wives and the household jobs. You may well know of at least one unfortunate man who did not live long after his sudden cut off from the world of work. I have known several and will tell you about one desperately sad one.

This particular man had worked for the same employer for most of his working life and he retired on his 65th birthday. At 4.30 on his last day a director made a speech and handed over his leaving present. He said goodbye to his friends and at 5.30, half an hour after his normal time, he left the building. A few yards down the road he collapsed and died. What a tragedy and it was a tragedy that left a question with big financial consequences for his widow. Did he die whilst employed or did he die during his retirement? If it was the former, his widow was due a significant life-assurance payout in addition to a widow's pension. If he died in retirement, she only qualified for the widow's pension. What do you think? The answer is given in the footnote at the end of this chapter.

Helpful character traits and attributes

I approach this part of the chapter with some caution. This is because in my experience, and very probably in yours too, people with a wide range of character traits and attributes make a success of their business. Sometimes a person lacking many of the qualities usually considered necessary will do well. This may be because he or she has one or more of the others in abundance. Nevertheless, it is possible to identify factors that are very likely to be helpful. The following are based on my own experience and observations, and many are confirmed by the views of other writers on the subject.

Self-motivation

Self-motivation is the most important of motivators and it helps achieve success in many walks of life, including paid employment. Of course we may all be motivated by money and such things as the wish to earn the respect of our family, friends and neighbours, but if you are an employee, your motivation may partly be drawn from your bosses and your colleagues. When you are self-employed the prop of your bosses and colleagues is absent. You must rely on self-motivation. If it is lacking, you will be in trouble. Of course if your business has (or acquires) partners and staff, they may be a source of motivation.

Self-confidence

Arrogance, which is an unjustified high opinion of our importance and abilities, is not good, but you should believe in yourself – in general, but in particular you should have the justified belief that you have the qualities to make a success of the business. It has been noted that others often accept our own valuation of ourselves and that they are right to do so. What is more, they often have the knack of spotting what our valuation of ourselves is, even if we try to disguise it. If you have confidence in yourself, customers and others may well follow your lead.

Self-discipline

Self-discipline is not the same as self-confidence, though it has a lot in common with self-motivation. Employees probably have discipline imposed upon them. In some cases it is a great deal of discipline and they have little or no say in their timekeeping and working practices. In others it may be less, though there will always be some. If you are self-employed, you must impose the discipline on yourself. No-one will do it for you and it matters very much. It comes naturally to some and is very difficult for others. You do not have to make a prompt start and you can have long holidays and early finishes. You can neglect the business and take your eye off the ball. It is up to you, but you will see the result in the bottom line of the profit and loss account.

Some years ago a colleague of mine left to start his own business and after a few months he came back to see us. We spent a most enjoyable hour over a pub lunch and at 2.00 pm, as the most senior person present, I said that we would give it another 20 minutes before going back to the office. He politely declined by telling us that he had a very demanding boss who would not understand his not being on the job. I have never forgotten it and I have never forgotten that he made a great success of his business.

The right attitude to hard work

It is sometimes said that success is 10 per cent inspiration and 90 per cent perspiration. I would not accept this exact split but sheer hard work will almost certainly get you a long way. The lazy will be at a very big disadvantage. A very few businesses may succeed because of the brilliance of an idea or the absence of competition, though these advantages will probably only be temporary. In nearly all cases hard work is an essential prerequisite of success.

It is easy to underestimate the demands that will be placed upon your time and, if you are used to working for an employer, how much you might miss the in-house services. There will not be a finance department, a lawyer, an IT department or any of the other specialists. You must do things yourself or pay to have them done.

Persistence and resilience

Many successful people will tell you that they had to knock on a lot of doors before they achieved success, and they may add that even after their success they had to overcome many subsequent setbacks. Unlike their unsuccessful competitors they were persistent and did not give up. You will face many disappointments and must press on regardless. In the words of the song, you must 'pick yourself up, dust yourself down and start all over again.'

Resilience has much in common with persistence. It will help if you are able to take the inevitable knocks without it affecting you too much. Ideally you should not get downhearted and you should be able to mentally switch-off when you are not working. Many self-employed people find this particularly hard to do.

Optimism

Do you think that a glass is half full or half empty? A generally optimistic disposition, so long as it is tempered with realism, will be a great help. Blind optimism is not good but a tendency to expect a positive outcome, unless there are reasons for a contrary view, most certainly is.

Decisiveness

It will be helpful if you are a person who makes clear decisions promptly. This will inspire respect from customers, suppliers and the world in general. Of course, being decisive is not the same as being impulsive and a poor early decision may be worse then a delayed better decision. We all respect people who do not duck awkward situations and give a firm response. It is true in business too.

An ability to organise

Whatever the nature of your self-employment you will need to organise the work that you do and your business in general. In some jobs and the profession of accountancy is a good example, this is extremely important. In others it is not so vital, but it still matters. As well as doing the job you need to organise your day, keep on top of the paperwork and do such things as make appointments and keep them on time. This will contribute to the success of your business. Working in a muddle will make things difficult.

It is no coincidence that self-motivation is mentioned first in the list of attributes, that the first three include the word 'self' and that all of them home in on what sort of person you are and how you operate.

You may have the benefit of help and advice, but it is you, your character traits and attributes that will be critical. It is extremely unlikely that you will have all the attributes mentioned. If you have, you will probably already have achieved a great deal and it is unlikely that you will read this book. It really is important that you are self-motivated and the more of the attributes that you have the better. One or two very strongly present may compensate for the missing ones. For example, a self-motivated person who works very hard may get away with a weakness relating to an ability to organise.

In my opinion it is not necessary that you are an extrovert, though it is no bad thing to be. Many introverts are competent and very self-motivated, and they are suited to self-employment. A friendly introvert often does well, though as both my wife and I (in our opinions) come into this category, perhaps this is a biased opinion.

Can you afford to take the risk?

No-one starts a business expecting it to fail, but what if it did? It is only being prudent to try and quantify the risk and consider if you are in a position to take it.

An obvious starting point is your own financial position. If you are wealthy or at least comfortably placed, perhaps the risk of failure need not trouble you unduly. So long as it is something that you want to do and you believe that there is a reasonable chance of success, go for it.

The next point to consider is your family and other responsibilities and commitments. If you are single or childless, or the children have left home and are doing well, it is probably reasonable to take a bigger risk than if this is not the case. Perhaps wives, husbands or other relatives depend on you. Perhaps you are expecting the Bank of Mum and Dad to help your children. Do you have a mortgage? What about inflexible outgoings? These are all things that should be taken into account.

You should recognise that some businesses are inherently more risky than others and also that some businesses require much more start-up capital than others. If you are considering working from home as a freelance proof reader, the start-up costs will probably be very small, perhaps just a few hundred pounds, and the cost if the venture does not succeed would probably also be small. On the other hand if you plan to open a new restaurant, the risk of failure may be higher than with many other businesses, and both the start-up costs and the write-off if the business fails are likely to be high.

The amount of risk will be influenced by the way that you intend to start the business. Many people do this whilst in full-time employment by working in the evenings and at weekends. This may well suit the freelance proof reader mentioned earlier. Only when income is being generated and the business is succeeding does the person make the full commitment and give up the day job. The risks would obviously be small. This way of starting would probably not be an option for the person planning to open a new restaurant. He or she would have to take a much bigger risk.

If you have given up the day job, there is a cost of failure that should not be overlooked. This is the loss of your previous income whilst you are working in your new venture. Let us say that you give up salary and benefits worth £50,000 a year and your new business folds after six months with losses of £40,000. The cost to you will have been £65,000, and you will probably not have a job at the end of it.

The chances of success

Various statistics are quoted, many of them with very dubious origins, contradictory and inaccurate, but it is sometimes said that around 400,000 businesses are started each year in the UK and that around 30 per cent of them fail within three years. At first sight and perhaps even at second sight this is awful, and perhaps bad enough to put you off the idea of starting a business. However, as with most averages and statistics the figures need examination and interpretation. You may have heard of the man with one foot in a bucket of boiling water and the other foot in a bucket of ice. On average he was comfortable.

The 400,000 new businesses include numerous extremely small enterprises. Some of them are little more than hobbies and many never really get going. There are certainly nothing remotely like 120,000 insolvencies each year (30 per cent of 400,000). What is meant by failure? Many of the businesses are discontinued with little or no loss of money, perhaps because their owners decide to pursue other opportunities or simply change their minds.

I can give a personal example of this. A friend was insecure and unhappy in his job and his applications to other employers were unsuccessful. He decided to set up a new business and I helped him form a company for this purpose. He had spent about a thousand pounds and was just about to start generating income when he was approached with an offer of a prestigious and very highly paid directorship. It was an offer so good that he could not refuse it, so he accepted and wound up his company. This business will be counted in the 30 per cent of failures, but he does not see it that way and neither do I.

It would of course be wrong to deny that a significant number of new businesses do fail and that the consequences can be serious for at least some of their owners. These consequences may be financial and they may include a dispiriting loss of morale. On the other hand, although always regrettable, they may not be serious and may even be trivial. Some businesses carry an inherently high degree of risk and some have an inevitably high demand for start-up capital. On the other hand, if you start a business as a self-employed window cleaner, the chances of success will be high (although the rewards may be relatively modest) and the consequences of failure not great.

In my opinion if a new business is well planned and if the proprietor has the right attributes and is well motivated, the chances of success are good.

Editorial comment

This chapter tries to fairly summarise the advantages and disadvantages of self-employment. Perhaps some of the disadvantages and attributes required will make you think very carefully and you might decide that it is not for you. If you do make this decision and it is the right decision for you, the price of this book has been money well spent. However, this chapter does not try to put you off, just to help you think, evaluate and make the right decision for you. Self-employment has been right for me and right for my wife, and we have no regrets. It may well be right for you too. Good luck to you, whatever you decide.

Our personal experiences

Both my wife and I think that we have many of the useful character traits and attributes listed in this chapter, though perhaps the views of people who know us well might be instructive. Our reasons for choosing self-employment were a mixture of most of the ones given, though we neither expected nor wanted vast riches. There was no need for Sir Philip Green to fear competition from us. A possible downside is that we have to watch the risk of our enjoyable jobs taking too big a part of our lives. Possibly this does sometimes happen.

My wife had the example of her father. After wartime service in the Royal Marines he vowed never to be in a position again where he had to take orders. From 1945 he had a number of businesses culminating in 35 years with his own driving school. He enjoyed it so much that he continued into his early eighties, teaching personally and always with a remarkably good pass rate. He never regretted opting for self-employment and he was possibly the oldest driving instructor in the country.

Footnote

(Answer to the question posed in this chapter)

Employment lasted until midnight on the last day. He therefore died whilst still an employee and his widow got the life assurance payment in addition to the widows' pension.

Chapter 2

Leaving your present employer

If you are not currently working for an employer, you might decide to bypass this chapter. I would understand but I suggest that you read it through anyway as it contains tips that you may find useful. It is probable that most people reading this book will currently be employed, perhaps feeling unsettled or perhaps facing the possibility or certainty of dismissal in the near or medium future. For you this is a vital chapter that should on no account be skipped. It may help you save a lot of money, contribute to your peace of mind and make it more likely that your business venture will get off to a flying start.

You should almost always try to leave your employer on good terms. There are numerous practical reasons why this will probably be to your advantage and many of them are explained in this chapter, but here is an extra one. Remember the old saying 'Be nice to people on your way up – you might meet them on the way down'. Of course your business is going to be a success and you will never want to work for your present employer again. You should believe this and it is probably true, but why burn your bridges?

Leaving on good terms might not be easy and you may want to tell the boss exactly where to stick his (or her) rotten job, but at least try to achieve a civilised departure. Apart from anything else this will give you the moral high ground and it might even be a satisfying put down for the boss. As well as the practical advantages, the sum of human happiness (including your own) is likely to be enhanced if you can manage it. You are probably a nice person (most people are) and the boss might be too. So give it a go. Having delivered this little homily I move on to the following topics which will be covered in this chapter:

- A good leaving
- Your employment contract and competing with your present employer
- Details of useful contacts
- Notice
- Our personal experiences

A good leaving

This paragraph is written on the premise that your employer is civilised and reasonable. If this is not the case, and you are probably in a position to know, you should perhaps not adopt the advice in this paragraph and keep your plans secret until you are ready to act. Having said that, there is a lot to be said for discussing your situation and options with your employer ahead of making the decision to leave and start your own business. A reasonable employer should respect your integrity and it may well help both of you. The conversation may result in the offer of promotion, a rise, an offer to resolve whatever the problem is or just conceivably all three. If this does happen, you might decide to abandon your plans and stay where you are. This has happened many times, but on the other hand the attractions of being your own boss may still be too great.

An unwelcome consequence of going it alone could possibly be a certain amount of isolation and loneliness. Staying in touch with your friends and present employer could go some way towards minimising this. Keep in touch after you have gone and meet up from time to time. As well as being enjoyable there may be business benefits, especially if your new business is in a similar sector to that of your employer. Best of all, your present employer could be a customer of your new business or sales leads could come your way, but in any case the news and gossip could be useful.

When starting up for yourself a sudden and total loss of secure income and complete dependence on your new business can be at best worrying and at worst frightening. This is particularly so if you have few savings and people depending on you. The prospect might even prevent you going alone. It is possible that your employer would let you go gradually, working part time or reducing your hours in stages. That way you would have some secure income whilst you build up your new business and start drawing an income from it. It is often said that the most successful negotiations finish with a win/win agreement that gives something to both parties. That should be your aim.

Your employment contract and competing with your present employer

You may have an employment contract that covers much more than the basics of pay, notice, holiday entitlement etc, and the more senior you are the more likely this is to be the case. Such a contract will probably try to restrict your ability to work for a competitor, compete with your present employer, entice work colleagues to leave and work for you, use confidential information and exploit knowledge and contacts acquired whilst working for them. The good news is that if these provisions are unreasonable, they are probably unenforceable.

When planning to leave your employer and start your own business you should, if you have an employment contract, at an early stage have a close look at it. What you should do next depends on your plans and what it contains. If there is nothing troublesome in it and if your business will not be local and will not compete with your employer, there may be nothing to worry about, but remember that your employer's opinion may not be the same as yours. My advice is that if you have any doubts at all, take suitable legal advice at an early stage. Know your rights and act accordingly. Legal action, bad feeling or both could be very expensive and time consuming. Your employer will almost certainly have more money and resources than you and could feel vindictive. If your contract and plans are straightforward, it should not cost too much and it could save a lot of grief. Not to take advice could be a false economy.

Fortunately, from your point of view, the courts may not enforce the provisions of a contract that amount to unreasonable restraint of trade. Numerous employers are blissfully unaware that the restraints in their employees' contracts are unenforceable and get a nasty shock when it is put to the test. Others are fully aware but try it on, thinking that they might get away with it. This supposition is sometimes justified. I cannot tell you in this book what amounts to unreasonable restraint of trade because it depends on individual contracts and circumstances, and possibly on the capriciousness of the court.

I can tell you that the shorter the period of restriction and the more narrowly that the restriction is drawn, the more likely that it will be upheld by a court. Take for example a driving instructor leaving a driving school in Exeter to set up his own driving school. A contract forbidding him from doing this for three months within ten miles of Exeter may well be enforceable, but a contract forbidding him from doing it for ten years in the counties of Cornwall, Devonshire, Somerset and Dorset would not be enforceable. However, circumstances may alter cases. A driving school has many thousands of potential clients. A person working for an employer with only a handful of potential clients in the whole country may be in a different position. If in doubt, seek legal advice.

Finally, just because you cannot sell to a person for a period it does not mean that you cannot (with care) talk to them and prepare the ground for future business.

Details of useful contacts

Some employers may not be happy with the following advice, but this book is intended to help you, not them. It is a good idea to compile a list of friends and potentially useful contacts, both within your employer and outside, together with such details as their addresses, telephone numbers and e-mail addresses. These may be useful at some stage and perhaps sooner rather than later. Your employer may try to stop you doing this and it is not unknown for staff, particularly sales staff, to be escorted off the premises within minutes of their resignation being handed in or being informed of their termination. The way of defeating this is of course to compile the details before your resignation is known, and also to do it if you suspect that the termination of your employment may soon be initiated by your employer.

Notice

If you resign you are required to give your employer the period of notice stipulated in your contract (or in the absence of a contract the statutory period of notice according to your length of service) and to work it. It is possible that your employer might agree to less notice, but this is at the employer's discretion. Occasionally a person leaving will unilaterally refuse to work the required period of notice. This is a breach of the employment contract and the employer could seek damages, though in practice this rarely happens. It is an unfair thing to do and most definitely does not conform with the advice to try and leave on good terms. I do not recommend it.

If your employment is terminated by your employer and except in a case of gross misconduct, you are entitled to the period of notice stipulated in your contract (or in the absence of a contract the statutory period of notice according to your length of service) and are required to work it. Your employer may ask you not to work your period of notice but the required period must nevertheless be paid. This applies to redundancy as well as termination for other reasons, and the redundancy payment will be in addition to the period of notice. If you believe that your termination is unfair dismissal, you can bring a case to the employment tribunal.

A marvellous outcome, from your point of view, is to have all your plans for self-employment in place, then to be dismissed by your employer and the dismissal to be accompanied by a payment in lieu of notice and perhaps some further pay-off. Needless to say this is not easy to achieve.

Our personal experiences

Both my wife and I have successfully followed the advice given in this chapter. Some years ago my wife left her employment as a Deputy Registrar of Births, Marriages and Deaths in order to become a self-employed Civil Funeral Celebrant. She left with everyone's good wishes and we have remained friends with her colleagues and manager.

In 1997 I was fired in the circumstances outlined in the introduction to this book. I departed with the friendship and good wishes of my colleagues and we kept in touch afterwards. The man who (foolishly in my opinion) fired me did it in a civilised way and I responded in kind. We helped each other in one or two ways and he later employed me to do a few days work with the company's pension fund.

Perhaps my good humour about my dismissal was influenced by the fact that I managed to do what I describe in the 'Notice' section of this chapter. I had been very unhappy and had completely prepared my plans for self-employment. I was dismissed with a payment in lieu of the long period of notice stipulated in my contract. I was able to leave at 5.30 on Friday and hit the ground running at 9.00 on Monday. I realise that this makes me sound a little smug, but it is what happened.

Chapter 3

Some fundamental early decisions

This chapter will help you decide whether to buy an existing business or sign up to a franchise, rather than starting from scratch. It will also examine the pros and cons of working from home and conclude by helping you decide the most suitable legal form for your business. Topics covered are:

- Buying an existing business

- Franchise

- To work from home or not to work from home?

- The most suitable legal form for your business
  - Sole trader
  - Limited company
  - A partnership
  - Limited Liability Partnership (LLP)

- Our personal experiences

Buying an existing business

Much of this book advises on starting a business from scratch, but there is of course the alternative of making the move into self-employment by buying an existing business. This may suit someone in a hurry and with capital, and there may be other reasons too. One of them could be that, so long as you do your homework and choose carefully, you will be getting something that you know works. It will have a good business model and deliver predictable, satisfactory results. On the other hand it may not be doing this and you might believe that you can do better. If it is not doing well, you should be able to get it cheaply and this may make it attractive.

There are a number of things that can go wrong. You will probably be buying goodwill and the benefits could turn out to be illusory. Some customers may not transfer their loyalty to you in the way that you expect, especially if they had a particular bond with the previous owner. This can apply to staff as well. Either or both might resent changes that you intend to make.

It is important to know why the present owner is selling and it might not be easy to find out, although the reason may seem obvious and indeed be obvious. Such things as death, illness and retirement come to mind, but regardless of what you are told there might be something known to the seller but not to you. This could be, for example, a forthcoming development in the trade that will make the business uncompetitive, or the impending arrival of a powerful competitor.

Businesses for sale are widely advertised in newspapers, suitable publications and websites. Two of the many useful websites are www.daltonbusiness.com and www.uk.businessesforsale.com. When you have located a serious prospect the next stage is to look at the premises, stock and assets (if any) and ask numerous questions. What these questions are will depend on the business and individual circumstances. You will certainly want to see several years accounts, if they exist. They may not be audited but you will probably take some comfort if they have been prepared by a reputable accountant.

You will almost certainly involve an accountant and a solicitor to advise you. This will add to the cost but it would very probably be a false economy not to do so. The accountant will advise on interpreting the accounts and suggest (if relevant) searching questions on such matters as stock valuation and the adequacy of the bad debt reserve. Do not forget that a person planning to sell a business has an obvious incentive to adopt the most favourable view on such matters. The solicitor will also suggest questions and may advise on such things as leases and staff employment contracts. It may seem tedious and could irritate the seller, but it is for your benefit.

How should a business be valued? This is an inevitable question and one to which it is impossible to give a definitive answer. Unless it is a forced sale (and arguably even then) a business is worth what a willing buyer is willing to pay to a willing seller. What it ought to be worth is not of major consequence. This is something that you must remember if you seek to sell a business at some time in the future. Having said that, the following are indications of two possible methods of valuation. You and your advisers must decide which one is most appropriate, or decide to reject both of them and proceed in a completely different way.

Asset-based method

As the name suggests, this method takes account of the value of the assets being acquired and it is obviously of most relevance when the assets are significant. You must decide whether it is realistic to value the assets at book value or whether some other basis should be adopted. If used in isolation, this method takes no account of goodwill and future profits.

Earnings-based method

This method uses a multiple of the net profits as the basis. It is usual to add back depreciation, interest, the salary or drawings of the owner and tax. The chosen multiplier is used and fixed assets added to the result. For example:

Annual profit after adding back depreciation, interest, the salary or drawings of the owner and tax	£30,000
Chosen multiplier	4
Fixed assets	£15,000

The valuation would be £120,000 (4 x £30,000) + £15,000 = £135,000. Put another way the valuation would be the value of the fixed assets plus four times the annual earnings. It is obviously important that the £30,000 figure be reliable, typical and sustainable. It could, for example, be the average of the last three years results. It may be unrealistically high if the owner has used creative accounting to make the last year's profit look good. There is another possibility that should perhaps in a few cases be considered. It is not unknown for owners or staff to surreptitiously (and illegally) extract cash from a business without putting it through the books. This has the effect of depressing the stated profits below the true figure. If this has been done, the business may be worth more than the formula would indicate.

After reaching a view on an acceptable valuation of the business the next step will be to negotiate with the seller. It is likely, but not certain, that the seller will be asking for a price higher than he or she is willing to accept, rather as a person selling a house may be willing to consider offers. This is a matter for negotiation and it is probable that your solicitor and accountant will make a valuable contribution. The seller will be receiving advice in the same way. Your advice will not be to agree the price, which has to be a matter for you, but to advise and help structure the deal fairly and to your advantage. For example, the contract may require the seller to give certain warranties, and part of the payment may be deferred and made conditional on projected profit figures being achieved.

Franchise

The British Franchise Association and many franchisors claim lustily that franchising can be very attractive, that the failure rate is less than for business start-ups in general and that bank finance may be more readily available than for business start-ups in general. All these claims can be true and a franchise may deserve serious consideration, though there can be problems that should not be overlooked.

There are more than 800 franchises available in the UK and you will certainly recognise some of the names. Prontaprint, Thorntons, McDonald's and Body Shop come readily to mind and there are many more. The investment required may be as much as several hundred thousand pounds for a major outlet for a very well known franchisor, but it can be less than £10,000 in some cases.

One advantage of a good and well-chosen franchise is that you become part of a proven operation that is known to work well, has high customer recognition and is very likely to deliver a satisfactory supply of sales leads and customers. The package gives you training, a helpline, stock (if appropriate), systems and much more. You pay a fee to join and an annual royalty that will probably be a percentage of your profit or turnover. You will probably get the exclusive right to operate in a defined territory.

One possible disadvantage is the converse of the advantages of the standard package. You will be required to strictly conform with the requirements of the franchise. You may have to wear a standard uniform and must set prices, buy stock, advertise, market your business etc as specified in the agreement. You will rapidly be reminded of this if, for example, you have a McDonald's franchise and decide that the ubiquitous logo would be more effective in purple rather than yellow. At best this may be irksome, even if it works well, and at worst it may stop you doing things that you correctly believe will help you improve your business. Something may work well in one part of the country but not in another. You should also remember that your exclusive territory will not protect you from competitors outside the franchise. For example, a McDonald's franchise will not be protected from a new outlet of Kentucky Fried Chicken.

It is probably worth getting information from the British Franchising Association (www.thebfa.org). It is the franchisors' body but you may well find it very useful. Another very useful source of information is the Approved Franchise Association (www.theafa.org.uk). Do talk to several franchisors and compare them. Do a lot of research and talk to a number of existing franchisees. Try to ensure that the franchisor is well-established, reputable and well-financed. You should be able to rely on them to deliver their side of the bargain in bad times as well as in good. It is strongly recommended that you use a lawyer with a special knowledge of franchises.

To work from home or not to work from home?

This is a key decision that must be made before commencing business, though a halfway house is starting from home with the intention or possibility of later moving to business premises. Of course for some the question does not arise because the nature of the business makes it very difficult or impossible to work from home. A shop obviously comes into this category and so may a manufacturing business or a business that requires a lot of storage space. It would also not suit a business that will make a lot of noise or otherwise be a nuisance to the neighbours, to say nothing of attracting the displeasure of the planning authorities.

On the other hand working from home is feasible for many venturing into self-employment, and technological advances are making it more and more common. This goes hand in hand with the trend for more employed people to work partly or wholly from home. Why then are commuter trains still so crowded? It is one of life's great mysteries. Examples of people who successfully work from home are consultants and professional people such as accountants. It may be easier for people who work from home but are out a lot, such as electricians. The following are some of the advantages and disadvantages:

Advantages

• It will probably save a lot of money.
• It will save the time and money spent travelling to and from work.

- Some home expenses can legitimately be charged against the business. Details are given in Chapter 10.

Disadvantages

- It will reduce the living space available to you and your family.

- It may put a strain on family life.

- It may not give the professional image that you want to convey.

- It may be difficult to keep home life and family life separate.

So long as your home activities are not excessive it is unlikely that you will have to pay business rates. You must tell your insurance company that you are working from home as failure to do so could invalidate your house and contents policies. There will probably not be a problem but you must tell them. If members of the public will visit you at home, you should take out public liability insurance. You should tell your mortgage provider, if this is applicable. All these requirements are frequently disregarded and usually no harm results, but they should nevertheless all be done.

The following seven pieces of advice are designed to help you if you do decide to work from home. They are drawn from my experience and the experience of others, and are worth serious consideration.

1. You should try to have a separate office or work area. I realise that this may be difficult but it makes a big difference. It may be possible to work from a garage or shed, or even have a separate office or outside building specially built. If you have a very long memory indeed you may remember a television series called The Larkins starring David Kossoff. His American son-in-law was a

writer who, in an entertaining way, regularly screamed at the family because he could not work without distractions. This illustrates the need for a separate work area.

2. You must try to make friends and family realise that you are at work. They will think that you are available for socialising and errands, and distract you accordingly. You should tell them that interrupting you is the equivalent of interrupting you when you worked for an employer. If they would not have done it then, they should not do it now. In the case of family you might add that the money that you are earning is partly for their benefit. It will not be easy and you will have to keep doing it.

3. You should have a separate telephone and ensure that it is answered efficiently. Callers may be enchanted by a child answering a business call, but they might not.

4. If business visitors will come to your home, steps should be taken to make their experience as impressive as possible in the circumstances. It will not be good for business if visitors are frightened by a dog and distracted by a television blaring in the next room. For an occasional important visitor it might be worth hiring a meeting room or arranging to meet in an impressive hotel. A friend regularly meets clients over coffee and biscuits in five star London hotels. It is good for business, both he and the client enjoy it and the cost is tax-deductible.

5. You should decide a sensible division between work hours and non-work hours and try to keep to it.

6. Clients, customers and other business contacts should know what your working hours are and should be discouraged from contacting you outside them. Some still will of course. It helps having a

separate business telephone number and you can put a business-like recorded message on this when your working hours are over. It is probably what would happen if you worked for an employer, but you should not be so ruthless that you drive away trade. It might be a fine line.

7. If you have a separate office or work space, put reasonably good quality furniture in it, especially if you expect to spend a lot of time there. It will improve your life and probably your work too.

The most suitable legal form for your business

You could just start trading without giving any thought to the legal form that your business will take. This would make you a sole trader, which is very common and could be your best choice. Nevertheless, it is worth studying the various possibilities and considering the pros and cons of each. The following are the four most common options and are examined in detail.

Sole trader

This is the option taken by the majority of people who start a business. It has the merit of simplicity and the minimum of regulation, compliance and bureaucracy. You can in most cases just get going. It is important though that you notify HM Revenue and Customs within three months of starting, and register for VAT if your likely turnover is above the threshold or if it is in your interest to register voluntarily. Advice on this is given in Chapter 10. Although you can just start working it is very much in your interests to get the basics right – for example, having suitable stationery printed and organising a proper bookkeeping system. As a self-employed person your profits will be subject to income tax rather than corporation tax.

A significant disadvantage of being a sole trader is that you do not have the benefit of limited liability. This means that you are responsible for any losses and debts incurred by the business. This really does mean that your house and other assets are at risk, and that in the last resort you could be made bankrupt.

Limited company

A limited company is a legal entity that can sue and be sued in its own name, and it is distinct from its shareholders and directors who may or may not be the same people. As the name suggests it gives you the benefit of limited liability, and furthermore the liability can be limited to a very small amount. This gives you the considerable benefit of protecting your house and other personal assets if the business fails. If this happens, the amount that you have paid for your shares is lost but, assuming that the shares were fully paid, you have no further responsibility. This is, of course, in the absence of fraud. The amount of the share capital can be and often is, a nominal sum. 85 per cent of companies have an issued share capital of £100 or less. As a no doubt honourable person you might feel under a moral obligation to pay at least some of the creditors in the event of your business failing, but this is not a legal requirement. In practice limited liability might not be quite all that it seems. This is because banks, understandably, are likely to want security or personal guarantees before lending to a poorly financed company. Some suppliers might also ask for personal guarantees.

There is a certain cost and a certain amount of work in setting up a limited company, though less than is often supposed. You could register a new company at Companies House yourself, though this would almost certainly not be a good idea. Much better would be to buy an off the shelf company that has never traded from a company formation agent. This is likely to cost no more than £50 and you would get a 'bog standard' limited company with the name you want, yourself as director and a registered office address of your choosing. You could make any further changes yourself (to the articles for example) or the agent would do it for a fee. The website of the Association of Company Registration Agents is www.acra-uk.org and this gives a list and contact details of company registration agents who are members of it. Alternatively, for a larger, though probably not unreasonable charge, an accountant or solicitor would do the whole thing and give you exactly the company you want.

It is possible to have a truly one-person company. You can be the sole shareholder and sole director, and you do not have to have a company secretary. Subject to conditions and in the likely event that annual turnover is not more than £6,500,000, you do not have to have an audit. Unless you are well-informed there are risks in all this. It may be sensible to involve a professional such as an accountant or solicitor, perhaps as company secretary.

You have to send statutory accounts (usually annually) to Companies House and an annual return. Companies House makes no charge for the accounts but there is a filing fee of £14 for the annual return if it is submitted electronically. The charge is £40 if it is submitted on paper rather than electronically. You will probably have to pay to have your accounts prepared in the manner required for a limited company. Certain other documents may have to be filed at Companies House from time to time.

Having a limited company is a privilege and in return for that privilege you will be required to make a certain amount of information available to the public at Companies House. You no longer have to reveal the residential address of the directors, but other personal information must be given, date of birth and any former names for example. Your balance sheet and certain other information is available but, if it is a small company (up to £6,500,000 annual turnover subject to conditions) the profit figure does not have to be disclosed.

The company will pay corporation tax on its profits. You will pay income tax on the salary and dividends that you take from the company. There may be advantages in this because national insurance contributions are not payable on dividends, and also because you can time your salary and dividends. You can, for example, choose to smooth out good years and bad years, and perhaps avoid paying higher rate income tax in a good year. More details are given in Chapter 10.

There may be a further advantage in having a company. Many people think that a limited company has more status than a sole trader and some companies prefer to trade with companies. This really is extraordinary. Why should Roger Mason Limited, with limited liability and £100 share capital, be more respected than Mr Roger Mason, who is trading as a sole trader with unlimited liability? Nevertheless it is a common perception.

A Partnership

A general partnership has two or more partners acting together in a business capacity. They do not have to register the business (except with HM Revenue and Customs) and each partner pays income tax. The partnership can be structured in various ways. Perhaps all the partners work full-time in the business, but perhaps one is a sleeping partner who has provided funds but has little other involvement.

The personal relationships and the strengths and weaknesses of each partner are very important. Ideally the partners should get on well, all work hard, respect each other and have complementary strengths. For example, a person who is good with finance might form a good partnership with someone who is good at selling. Being cynical, unsuccessful partnerships can be bad for friendships, family relationships and even marriages.

It is not essential to have a formal partnership agreement, but it is strongly recommended. Some partners work informally sharing everything 50/50, which is fine until they fall out or something goes wrong. There should be a formal partnership agreement drawn up with legal advice. This may or may not be a long and detailed document, but it should cover such things as:

- How much capital does each partner put in?

- How are profits and losses divided?

- How are decisions made and what happens if the partners do not agree?

- How much work does each partner contribute?

- What happens when a partner wants to leave the partnership?

Each partner has joint and several personal liability for partnership debts, even if they were incurred by another partner. This should be cause for very serious thought.

Limited Liability Partnership (LLP)

A limited liability partnership has many of the features of a company, but it is a partnership with the flexibility that this confers. The partners pay income tax on their share of the profits. A major attraction is that, unlike a general partnership, the partners have limited liability, and are only liable for the amount that they have agreed to contribute if the partnership goes into insolvent liquidation.

A limited liability partnership must be registered at Companies House, and accounts and other information must be supplied to Companies House in the same way as a limited company.

Limited liability partnerships have their uses but limited companies are much more numerous. Most readers of this book are likely to prefer limited companies.

Our personal experiences

Neither my wife nor I have ever owned a franchise or bought an existing business. I have though several times advised on buying a business. On one occasion a colleague's wife asked for my advice when she was considering buying a shop. She had fallen in love with both the location and the products that it sold. I told her that it would have a detrimental effect on her family life, that the figures were horrific and that she would inevitably make a significant loss. She thanked me for the advice and bought it anyway. A year later she sold it because it was having a detrimental effect on her family life and had made a significant loss. I could say that this shows the soundness of my judgment, but my conclusion was so obvious that it would be wrong to make this claim. It would perhaps be fairer to admit a deficiency in my powers of persuasion.

Both my wife and I work from home and neither of us follows all of the advice in this chapter. I in particular disregard a lot of it. When I started I fixed my business hours, resolved to wear smart clothes in business hours, rigidly separated home life and business life and decided not to open Saturday's business post until Monday. All of this lasted about four days. I then abandoned it all and adopted the lifestyle that I have followed ever since.

I semi-work seven days a week and to a great extent mingle my business life with my family and social life. I take a lot of holidays and often take time out during the day, and I adopt different lifestyles from day to day. I am very disciplined when necessary but on other days I sometimes start work at 5.00 am and sometimes at 10.00 am. I often do relatively little in the day and work in the early morning and evening. Overall it adds up to a full commitment, possibly too full a commitment. It sounds a recipe for disaster but I enjoy it and it works very well for me. It would not be right for many other people, so perhaps you had better follow the advice in this chapter.

Chapter 4
Available advice and information

There is a lot of advice and information available, and some of it is described in this chapter. However, we begin with some matters of general application.

A useful starting place is to make the fairly obvious point that not all professional advisers are equally good. Furthermore, they do not all charge the same and some are even free. It is therefore important to choose your advisers carefully. You will certainly want people who are technically sound and they should be reasonably available when you want them. They should be advisers that you trust and preferably people with whom you get along. You can talk to more than one person before making a choice. A personal recommendation by someone already in business could be an excellent starting point.

Very large firms of solicitors and accountants for example are likely to be much more expensive than small firms or sole practitioners. You may be paying for specialised expertise that you do not actually need, and you may finish up dealing with an inexperienced person, rather than the great man or great woman.

Charging can be a fraught subject, so you need to know and agree at the outset the basis on which you will be charged. Depending on what will be done for you it could be an agreed fixed sum. This could be suitable for such things as preparing the quarterly VAT return, but on the other hand the amount of work may not be exactly predictable, so you may need to agree an hourly rate or a range of charges.

Time is money. It is an old saying and you probably know the truth of it. If not, you will when your business gets going. It is true for advisers as well and they are entitled to charge for the use of their time. It therefore pays to not take up more of it than necessary. You should prepare for your meetings so that they do not take longer than is required.

You should remember that advisers are just that. They give advice and it is up to you whether you follow the advice. You mostly will, presumably, but it is your business and rightly the final decision is yours.

This chapter spotlights the following advisers:

- Business Link
- Enterprise Agencies
- Accountants
- Solicitors
- Banks

Business Link

Business Link was set up by the government department BIS and is supported by other government departments. There are Regional Business Links throughout England and equivalent organisations elsewhere in the United Kingdom. SMEs (small and medium-sized enterprises) are able to make direct contact with Business Link. Initial contact details are as follows:

Business Link (England)

Tel: 0845 600 9 006

www.businesslink.gov.uk

Business Gateway (Scotland)

Tel: 0845 609 6611

www.bgateway.com

Highlands and Islands Enterprise

Cowan House

Inverness Retail and Business Park

Inverness IV2 7GF

Tel: 01463 234171

www.hie.co.uk

Business Eye/Llygad Busnes (Wales)

Tel: 08457 96 97 98

www.businesseye.org.uk

Invest Northern Ireland

0800 181 4422

www.investni.com

Business Link offers advice on all aspects of business start-up s and it provides full information on a range of services. The website www.businesslink.gov.uk is very useful. You can enter your data into this website and you will be directed to your local Business Link. You will then be directed on to the help that you need. This can come from a range of sources including, and especially, a local Enterprise Agency.

Enterprise Agencies

Enterprise agencies help pre start-up businesses and very small businesses. They are independent organisations, not agencies of government, and they obtain their funding from a variety of sources, often including local authorities, banks etc. They receive many referrals from Business Link.

If you are accepted by an Enterprise Agency, you will be assigned a business adviser to help you. Staff have a wide knowledge of grants that may be available and may put you in touch with other appropriate business advisers. The staff are generally experienced and they have a high reputation. Some have run businesses. Some are seconded from local banks, companies, accountancy practices etc.

There are many local enterprise agencies and it may be worth checking out the National Federation. Contact details are:

National Federation of Enterprise Agencies
12 Stephenson Court
Fraser Road
Priory Business Park
Bedford MK44 3WH
Tel: 01234 831623
www.nfea.com

Accountants

A good accountant should be an invaluable source of good advice. This is most likely to be true if the advice involves money and figures, things such as tax, cashflow and book-keeping being obvious examples. Also, he or she should be able to contribute to the decision on the form that your business should take. As well as advising on setting up the business, the advice and the relationship should continue over the succeeding years. Of course a good accountant should have wide experience and be well connected, so may be able to advise in a more general way and introduce you to other suitable professionals.

It is often said that accountants are inherently cautious and there is often some truth in this. Perhaps it is because of their experience in sorting out business failures. This may be a good thing, so long as their attitude makes you resolved and realistic, and not defeatist and depressed.

It is also often said that accountants are often introverts, which is less true in my experience. My son and I are both accountants, so I feel able to share a light-hearted question that he put to me. He asked how you could tell that a man was an accountant. He then said that it was because when he was talking to you he would look at your shoes rather than at your face. He went on to say that the only person more introverted than an accountant is an actuary. When talking to you an actuary will look at his own shoes rather than your shoes.

You must decide whether to seek advice from a qualified accountant or an unqualified one. To the annoyance of qualified accountants there is no protection for the term 'accountant'. There is nothing to stop a failed tattooist setting up in business and calling himself an accountant, though unqualified accountants cannot do statutory audits and certain other things. Some unqualified accountants are good, at least for some things, and some are dreadful. Most are somewhere in between and of course they are likely to be cheaper than qualified accountants. If you do decide to use an unqualified accountant, you should be cautious and probably pick one who is well established. If possible the person should be recommended by someone whose judgment you trust.

Qualified accountants are members of professional bodies and you will have the protection and professional standards that are a consequence of this. You should be confident of good work on your behalf.

There are a number of accountancy bodies and all will be pleased to advise on qualified members in your area. You could approach one of the following.

Association of Chartered Certified Accountants

2 Central Quay

89 Hydepark Street

Glasgow G3 8BW

Tel: 0141 582 2000

www.acca.co.uk

Institute of Chartered Accountants in England and Wales

PO Box 433

Moorgate Place

London EC2P 2BJ

Tel: 0207 920 8100

www.icaew.co.uk

Institute of Chartered Accountants in Ireland

CA House, 83 Pembroke Road

Dublin 4

Republic of Ireland

Tel: (00 353) 1 637 7200

www.icai.ie

Institute of Chartered Accountants of Scotland

CA House, 21 Haymarket Yards

Edinburgh EH12 5BH

Tel: 0131 347 0100

www.icas.org.uk

Solicitors

Solicitors, like accountants, can be a source of invaluable advice in many areas. These may include such things as property, leases, contracts, employment law and the best legal form for the business to take. They are usually meticulous, which is one of the things that you are paying for and, again like accountants, they can sometimes be very cautious. They are sometimes criticised for being slow, but this is often not their fault. A property transaction involves two parties and, like a convoy, it moves at the speed of the slowest party. It pays to have a clear idea of what you want and, if it is important, ask for speed.

Solicitors, unlike accountants, have protection for the name of their profession. A failed tattooist cannot set himself up in business and call himself a solicitor. The solicitors' professional body is the Law

Society and there are three of them, one for each of the constituent parts of the United Kingdom. Contact details are as follows:

The Law Society (England and Wales)

113 Chancery Lane

London WC2A 1PL

Tel: 0870 606 2555

www.lawsociety.org.uk

The Law Society of Northern Ireland

40 Linenhall Street

Belfast BT2 8BA

Tel: 028 9023 1614

www.lawsoc.ni.org

The Law Society of Scotland

26 Drumsheugh Gardens

Edinburgh EH3 7YR

Tel: 0131 226 7411

www.lawscot.org.uk

The Law Society (England and Wales) offers 'Lawyers For Your Business'. This is a network of 1,000 solicitor firms in England and Wales offering specialist advice to small and medium-sized businesses. They offer a free initial half hour consultation. Further details are on the website.

Banks

Many people starting a business approach a bank, often because they need to borrow money. Advice on approaching a bank for this purpose is given in Chapter 5 and advice on dealing with a bank on a continuing basis is given in Chapter 8.

A good personal relationship with a bank and a banker can be very useful and a source of very good and balanced advice. Your bank will undoubtedly wish you well and want you to succeed, not least because you will be a source of future business. An experienced banker will have seen a lot of start-ups and will have shrewd ideas about why some succeed and others fail. However, do not forget that he or she has probably not actually done it for themselves and, if push comes to shove, he or she will put the bank's interest first. You should also remember that banks have a strong interest in selling things to you. Keep in mind that you do not have to buy them and that equivalent products may be obtained more cheaply elsewhere.

Chapter 5

The business plan and break-even calculation

Some readers may find this the most difficult chapter in the book, but it is nevertheless important. Most of it is about your business plan, and for the reasons given near the beginning of the chapter you should have a good business plan. As someone once said 'Failing to plan is planning to fail'. The aspects covered are:

- What is a business plan?

- Should you prepare a business plan?

- Optimistic or pessimistic?

- Hints for the business plan

- The structure of your business plan

- Example of a business plan

- Break-even

- Our personal experiences

What is a business plan?

A business plan maps out how it is intended that the business will operate and its planned performance during the first period of its existence. The period chosen is often a year, but it is acceptable to pick a period of some other suitable length. Of course further plans and budgets can (and probably should) be done for subsequent periods after the business is up and running.

The plan should be partly a matter of figures and partly a matter of words. The figures should, at a minimum, detail the profit or loss of the business and also detail the cash coming in and going out. The words should set out the assumptions behind the figures. They should also identify what the business will do, set out key facts and assumptions, give details of the business model, the pricing strategy, the competition, limiting factors etc.

Businesses vary and accordingly suitable designs for business plans also vary, though I believe that my ideas set out in this chapter are suitable for most readers. Designing the layout will be part of the benefit of having a business plan.

Should you prepare a business plan?

The answer to the question is yes. It will almost certainly be essential if you need outside finance, and it will help you a lot whether or not this is the case. Formal planning on a computer or paper, rather than by instinct and mental calculation, has considerable advantages.

The benefits come from preparing the plan as well as using the end result. If you do it properly, you will set it out logically, confront problems, identify any limiting factors and find out how much finance you will need. By thinking things through in this way you may spot opportunities and improvements that had not previously occurred to you. Another benefit is that after you have started the business you will be able to measure your progress against the plan. So yes, you should prepare a business plan.

Optimistic or pessimistic?

Opinions are divided on this and each approach has its advocates. In favour of optimism it might be said that 'tough but achievable' would be a better phrase. If you make it too easy, you will not be challenging yourself and it may be less likely that you and the business will achieve your full potential. On the downside, failure to achieve the plan may be demotivating, and it might alarm the bank or anyone who you ask to lend you money. A too optimistic plan might persuade you to go ahead when it would be best not to do so, and it might leave you short of money later. The downsides do seem quite compelling and I do not recommend excess optimism. Pessimism would make it likely that you would achieve the plan, but it would be a rather meaningless achievement and there would not be a challenge. I do not recommend this either.

In many people's view, including mine, the plan should be realistic. Not everyone would agree but I would put in a few modest contingencies. These should be labelled as such and not achieved by inflating some of the figures. You should then go flat out to achieve the plan without needing the contingencies. This approach, so long as the results are acceptable, is likely to impress the bank or other lender.

Hints for the business plan

Different people have different ideas. These are some of mine.

1. I once failed to hand in some work at school and a master told me that if a thing is worth doing, it is worth doing badly. This is of course logically correct, but it is much better to do it well. Take the business plan seriously and do it well. You might not find it easy, but persevere. It will be worth it.

2. Software applications are marketed for the purpose of business plans. They may be good but do not get locked into an inappropriate structure. In any case, you can manage on your own. Banks provide suggested layouts.

3. An accountant or other professional will (for a fee) very probably do a good job for you. This may be sensible, but make sure that you 'own' it and that the end result is what you want. Do not let the tail wag the dog.

4. Make the finished product look impressive. Use good quality paper, head it properly and check for such things as spelling mistakes.

5. Do not forget the competition. It might improve and make things tougher for you. This was drummed into me very many years ago when I was a financial analyst with the Ford Motor Company. I was working on a plan and was instructed by my manager not to be too optimistic, and on no account to forget that British Leyland,

then going through a particularly bad patch, might improve and offer formidable competition. Of course this never actually happened. On the other hand my manager could sometimes be complacent. Around the same time imported Japanese cars went through a psychological barrier and took five per cent of the British market. He was quite gloomy and said that imported cars might take ten per cent of the market. Then he cheered up and said that cars made in Britain would always have a share of at least 90 per cent. Anything less than that was inconceivable.

6. Consider whether you will register for VAT and, if you will, factor it into the calculations, including the cash flow forecast.

7. Do not underestimate the importance of cash and do not underestimate the importance of timing. In the very long term cash and profit after tax may be the same, but as Maynard Keynes once remarked 'in the long term we are all dead'. In the short term profit and cash will almost certainly be significantly different. It is both possible and quite common for a profitable business to run out of cash, and even to have to close down. There are several reasons for timing differences, but consider a business that buys an article for £100 in January and pays for it in February, sells it on 60 day terms for £140 in May, but the customer takes an extra month to pay. There will be a gross profit of £40 but a cash outflow of £100 from February to August.

8. Do ask friends and business acquaintances for their opinions as you prepare the plan, and do ask for their opinions when the plan is finished. Obviously you will respect the views of some more than others, and do not on any account lose sight of the fact that it is your plan.

The structure of your business plan

The business plan for a major start-up, perhaps employing many people, may run to dozens of pages. On the other hand a small, one-person, simple start-up will be much more basic. The following lists the headings that would be suitable for both, but the plan for a small, simple start-up would contain much less. I commend it to you.

- Business summary

- Supporting information

- Products or services

- Marketing and sales information

- Running the business

- Start-up costs

- Cash flow plan

- Profit and loss plan

- Analysis of strengths, weaknesses, opportunities and threats

An accountant might project a forward balance sheet for you, but this may well not be necessary and may be beyond the skill of most people preparing a do-it-yourself plan.

A business manager at my bank told me that he would be surprised and delighted to be presented with a proposal and a business plan as described above. The great majority of what he gets is greatly inferior. He added that he agrees with Lord Sugar that the banks have money to lend. All that is required is a good proposal.

Let us move on to an outline review of each of the headings.

Business summary

As the title implies, this should be a concise summary of the proposed business venture. It needs to command attention and make the reader want to look at the rest of the plan, so it should be short, to the point and with each word well chosen. It probably should not be longer than half a page and could well be shorter. It should have a confident tone and tell the reader exactly what the business will be doing.

Supporting information

This is the section where you give information about yourself. It should contain concise personal information and details of any relevant professional qualifications and training, as well as brief details of your record in employment and (if applicable) self-employment.

Products or services

This section explains what you plan to sell to your customers. At its simplest it will just describe the products or services, but you should aim to show how they fit into the market and why there is a demand for what you will offer. You should refer to the competition and explain how your products or services will differ (if they will) and why you will succeed despite the competition. You should say why your products or services will be competitive – be it because of price, value, immediate availability, after sales service or some other reason.

Marketing and sales information

This is where you identify your target market and say how you intend to reach it. This will include selling, but the term 'marketing' goes much further and encompasses such things as advertising, direct mail, word of mouth and much more. If you are successful, you will achieve a high volume of sales for your products or services. You should say why this is believable and how it will be brought about.

Running the business

If you intend, for a time at least, to run a truly one-person operation, you should state this and explain how it will impact on your non-business life and how you will make any necessary arrangements. You will probably say whether you intend to work from home or have business premises. This sounds rather intrusive but it is important that you think it through. It will be of interest to a bank in the event that bank finance is requested.

If you intend to have partners, co-directors or employees (or some combination of them) details should be given, and you should outline the intended responsibilities and management structure. If people have already been recruited or identified, brief details should be given.

It might be a good idea to mention your expected relationship with any key suppliers, and to mention any other key factors.

Start-up costs

Start-up costs are the one-off items of expenditure that you will need to get started. Sometimes they are very small or possibly even non-existent, and some service businesses run from home may come into this category. Usually, though, there is at least some upfront expenditure. In a service business run from home it could, for example, include office furniture. In other cases significant amounts of capital may be required.

This section of the plan should list the start-up costs and they should be fed into the cash flow plan at or near the beginning. They should also be fed into the profit and loss plan as a charge against profit. If the start-up costs are revenue expenditure (an advertising campaign for example) the total costs should go in. If they are capital expenditure (a van for example) only part should go in. This is because they will be depreciated over a number of years.

Cash flow plan

The cash flow plan is explained before the profit and loss plan and there are reasons for this. One is that it helps construct the profit and loss plan, but another is its great importance. If you need to borrow money, your prospective lender will want to see a detailed, believable, projected running total of the amount required. You will certainly need the same information yourself, especially if you need to borrow money, but even if you do not.

Cash and profit are most definitely not the same thing. In the long run (ie when your business closes) cash and profit are the same thing, but in the short term they are most definitely not, and you have to pay your suppliers and feed your family in the short term. Failure to appreciate this and plan for it is a common mistake, and one that has led to numerous profitable or potentially profitable businesses folding.

Do not be among their number. The reasons for the timing differences between cash flow and profit include:

If, as will probably be the case, you supply goods or services on credit, you will have to wait for payment, but you will recognise the profit when you make delivery.

If, as will probably be the case, you buy goods or services on credit, you will make payment after charging the cost in the profit and loss account.

If you supply goods, you must finance the stock that you are holding.

If you make capital expenditure, cash must be found to pay for what you purchase. It will retain some of its value over a number of years and will be depreciated in the profit and loss account over a number of years.

The cash flow plan should give the figures in detail for each period, which is usually each month, and it should show the running total at the foot of each column. An example of a good layout is given in the example of a business plan later in this chapter. The figures should be supported by notes as appropriate.

Finally, when you use the cash flow plan, do not overlook the possibility of a peak borrowing requirement mid month. It is possible to need £20,000 at the end of July and £20,000 at the end of August, but to have a borrowing requirement of £30,000 on 15th August.

The profit and loss plan

Like the cash flow plan, the profit and loss plan is best set out in monthly columns, with all the columns adding across to the totals for the year or other period. A good specimen can be seen in the example of a business plan later in this chapter. The figures should be supported by notes as appropriate. Sometimes planned figures for a further year or two are added, probably totals only and not divided into monthly columns.

Analysis of strengths, weaknesses, opportunities and threats

This is sometimes abbreviated to 'SWOT Analysis'. It is a brief analysis of these four key features and how they might impact on the business. Planned action to exploit the strengths and opportunities might be mentioned, as might training or other action to counteract the weaknesses and threats. The following are examples of the things that might be included:

STRENGTHS

- Particular skills and experience that you have.
- Details of how you differ from the competition.
- Details of any perceived gaps in the market.

WEAKNESSES

- Any important and relevant weaknesses in your skills and experience. Your plans to cope with this could be for example:
  - hire the expertise needed
  - undergo training
  - do nothing and live with the problem
- Strong competition.

OPPORTUNITIES

- The expected failure or withdrawal of a competitor.

- An opportunity to do business with a major customer. Perhaps informal discussions have already taken place.

- The exploitation of a new market that has been recognised.

- The possibility of using the internet to liaise with customers and suppliers.

THREATS

- Possible price rises from suppliers that will be hard to pass on to customers.

- Your illness or unavailability for any reason.

- New competitors entering the market.

- Vulnerability to the loss of a key customer.

Example of a business plan

The following hypothetical example shows how someone starting up a one-person business as a sole trader might develop a business plan using the principles explained in this chapter. A relatively simple plan has been chosen because it should be easier to follow and because it is intended just to illustrate the principles.

Clive Green is 37 years old and will shortly be made redundant from his job in local government. He has decided to fulfil a long-standing ambition and set up his own business as a sole trader.

Clive is a keen gardener and his gardening knowledge and skills include expertise with turf and lawns. He intends to offer his services to maintain domestic lawns and grassy areas owned by businesses. This will be done mainly by signing customers up to annual contracts for specified treatments and care, with extra services available as required. He has done some basic market research and believes that there is a market for this, and that the competition is weak.

Clive intends to call his business 'SUPALAWN'.

Business summary

Under the trading name 'SUPALAWN' I will maintain domestic lawns and grass areas that are the responsibility of businesses. Most of the sales will be for annual contracts for periodic (usually quarterly) weeding, feeding and other maintenance, but a range of other services and treatments will also be available.

Supporting information

I am 37 years old, married and with two young children.

My entire career has been in the finance department of Buckinghamshire County Council. I joined at the age of 18 and progressed through a number of roles and departments. I am at present a section leader with a staff of two and my salary is £34,000 pa. I qualified as an Associate Member of the Institute of Accounting Technicians in 2008. My training and experience in finance and administration should ensure that these aspects of the business are run efficiently.

Gardening has been a lifelong interest and it has been my principal hobby. For this reason I have some considerable knowledge of the products and services that I will be supplying. I have for ten years been a member of Aylesbury and District Horticultural Society and am currently the president.

Services & products

Lawns and other areas of grass benefit enormously from four applications a year of fertiliser and weedkiller. This is commonly known as 'feed and weed' and the compounds used are varied according to the seasons. I will sign up customers for this on annual contracts, but with invoicing and payments due quarterly after each application. I anticipate that this will be my main source of revenue. I will also offer services on a one-off basis to deal with specific needs. This will include such things as scarifying and seeding, and dealing with specific problems and diseases. I intend to do everything myself for the first year then consider whether or not to employ staff.

The area in which I will operate has a number of contract gardeners but none of them specialise in lawns. There are two national franchises that offer the services that I will provide, but only one covers the geographical area in which I will operate. This is the only direct competition and my research indicates that customers and potential customers are dissatisfied with it. There is a feeling that it charges too much and that it is unreliable. I intend to set my prices approximately ten per cent lower and to offer a better service.

Marketing and sales information

130,000 people live within 15 miles of my home, which is where the business will be based. Many of the properties have significant lawns and some have very large lawns. It is a prosperous part of the country and many home owners can readily afford the services that I provide.

I intend to launch the business with a leaflet campaign and I intend that 3,000 carefully selected properties will receive a hand-delivered leaflet. I also intend to advertise in local newspapers during the first six weeks and cards will be placed in suitable shop windows. These cards (which are very cheap) will be maintained permanently. I am confident that repeat business and word of mouth will generate future orders, but I will consider repeat leaflets and advertising as and when necessary. I intend to take a stand at the Bucks County Show in August and I will have a website.

I intend to personally approach approximately 60 businesses and I have already spoken to seven. Two of these expressed interest and one put a firm intention in a letter, a copy of which is attached.

Running the business

I intend to run a one-person business for at least the first year, then consider taking on staff. I will work from home and my van, equipment and materials will all be stored in the large double garage and two large sheds. One of the bedrooms will be converted into an office. If and when I take on staff, it will be necessary to either take suitable premises or get the staff to store a van and equipment at their homes.

My wife is very supportive and would like to help, but she has a full-time job and will only be able to give a small amount of assistance. She will answer the telephone when she is available, but otherwise I will rely on a telephone answering machine. I will use a mobile phone and the number will be given in the leaflets and advertisements, and also made available to clients. I will do the administrative work myself.

The work on the grass will be done according to the weather and the seasons, and it will not usually be necessary to do it on a particular day or even a particular week. Taking short holidays should therefore not be a problem; and I will take the main family holiday at Christmas when no outside work is done.

There will not be any key suppliers and my materials can be obtained from a number of sources.

Start-up costs

START-UP COSTS

These will be as follows:

Capital expenditure

Van	£14,000
Spreader and other equipment	£6,000
Computer	£500
Office furniture	£2,500
	£23,000

Revenue expenditure

Printing and delivery of leaflets	£2,000
Advertising	£6,000
	£8,000

Cash flow plan and profit and loss plan

These plans follow. The notes relate to both plans and follow the profit and loss plan.

CASH FLOW PLAN

	May £	June £	July £	August £	September £	October £
Receipts						
Domestic customers	-	1,000	1,000	2,000	2,000	3,000
Business customers	-	-	300	500	600	600
	-	1,000	1,300	2,500	2,600	3,600
Payments						
Advertising and leaflets	2,000	2,000	4,000	50	50	50
Bucks County Show	-	-	-	500	-	-
Capital expenditure	20,000	3,000	-	-	-	-
Materials	-	100	200	200	200	250
Van running costs	100	200	300	300	300	300
Office expenses	50	50	50	50	50	50
Telephone and postage	80	80	80	80	80	80
Miscellaneous	200	200	200	200	200	200
Drawings	2,500	2,500	2,500	2,500	2,500	2,500
Interest	-	150	150	220	240	240
Contingency	100	100	100	100	100	100
	25,030	8,380	7,580	4,200	3,720	3,770
Excess of receipts over payments	(25,030)	(7,380)	(6,280)	(1,700)	(1,120)	(170)
Add opening requirement	-	(25,030)	(32,410)	(38,690)	(40,390)	(41,510)
Closing requirement	(25,030)	(32,410)	(38,690)	(40,390)	(41,510)	(41,680)

CASH FLOW PLAN

	November £	December £	January £	February £	March £	April £
Receipts						
Domestic customers	4,000	4,000	4,000	4,000	5,000	5,000
Business customers	600	600	600	600	800	800
	4,600	4,600	4,600	4,600	5,800	5,800
Payments						
Advertising and leaflets	100	100	100	100	100	100
Bucks County Show	-	-	-	-	-	-
Capital expenditure	-	-	-	-	-	-
Materials	300	350	350	350	400	400
Van running costs	400	400	400	400	400	400
Office expenses	50	50	50	50	50	50
Telephone and postage	100	100	100	100	100	100
Miscellaneous	200	200	200	200	200	200
Drawings	2,500	2,500	2,500	2,500	2,500	2,500
Interest	240	240	240	230	230	220
Contingency	100	100	100	100	100	100
	3,990	4,040	4,040	4,030	4,080	4,070
Excess of receipts over payments	610	560	560	570	1,720	1,730
Add opening requirement	(41,680)	(41,070)	(40,510)	(39,950)	(39,380)	(37,660)
Closing requirement	(41,070)	(40,510)	(39,950)	(39,380)	(37,660)	(35,930)

PROFIT AND LOSS PLAN

	May £	June £	July £	August £	September £	October £
Income						
Domestic customers	1,000	1,000	2,000	2,000	3,000	4,000
Business customers	-	300	500	600	600	600
	1,000	1,300	2,500	2,600	3,600	4,600
Expenditure						
Advertising and leaflets	4,000	4,000	50	50	50	50
Bucks County Show	-	-	-	500	-	-
Depreciation	480	480	480	480	480	480
Materials	100	200	200	200	250	300
Van running costs	100	200	300	300	300	300
Office expenses	50	50	50	50	50	50
Telephone and postage	80	80	80	80	80	80
Miscellaneous	200	200	200	200	200	200
Interest	-	150	150	220	240	240
Contingency	100	100	100	100	100	100
	5,110	5,460	1,610	2,180	1,750	1,800
Profit/(Loss) before drawings	(4,110)	(4,160)	890	420	1,850	2,800
Drawings	2,500	2,500	2,500	2,500	2,500	2,500
Profit/(Loss) after drawings	(6,610)	(6,660)	(1,610)	(2,080)	(650)	300

PROFIT AND LOSS PLAN

	November £	December £	January £	February £	March £	April £	Total Year £
Income							
Domestic customers	4,000	4,000	4,000	5,000	5,000	5,500	40,500
Business customers	600	600	600	800	800	800	6,800
	4,600	4,600	4,600	5,800	5,800	6,300	47,300
Expenditure							
Advertising and leaflets	100	100	100	100	100	100	8,800
Bucks County Show	-	-	-	-	-	-	500
Depreciation	480	480	480	480	480	480	5,760
Materials	350	350	350	400	400	400	3,500
Van running costs	400	400	400	400	400	400	3,900
Office expenses	50	50	50	50	50	50	600
Telephone and postage	100	100	100	100	100	100	1,080
Miscellaneous	200	200	200	200	200	200	2,400
Interest	240	240	240	240	230	220	2,410
Contingency	100	100	100	100	100	100	1,200
	2,020	2,020	2,020	2,070	2,060	2,050	30,150
Profit/(Loss) before drawings	2,580	2,580	2,580	3,730	3,740	4,250	17,150
Drawings	2,500	2,500	2,500	2,500	2,500	2,500	30,000
Profit/(Loss) after drawings	80	80	80	1,230	1,240	1,750	(12,850)

NOTES TO CASH FLOW PLAN AND PROFIT AND LOSS PLAN

- The business will not be registered for VAT during the first year.

- Customers will be invoiced immediately after each treatment is applied, not at the beginning of the contract period.

- It is assumed that customers will take an average of one month to pay.

- The invoice figures are net of bad debts, which are expected to be small.

- The fixed assets will be depreciated at the rate of 25% pa.

- My drawings of £2,500 per month will be the total amount that I take out of the business. I will pay the income tax and national insurance out of this.

- No provision is made for the tax on the profits and losses.

Analysis of strengths, weaknesses, opportunities and threats

STRENGTHS

- Genuine love of gardens and wish to help customers.

- Experience of finance and administration will be very helpful.

- A well thought-out plan and a strong motivation to succeed.

- High probability of repeat business.

WEAKNESSES

- No experience of self-employment.

- At times customers and potential customers will have to leave messages for me.

- I will be competing with a franchise that has high recognition.

OPPORTUNITIES

- I perceive that my major competition is weak and not well-respected.

- Many potential customers are not aware of the services that I (and my competitors) will provide.

- There is considerable scope to persuade customers who have signed for the basic package to take extra services, such as scarifying and seeding.

- There should be scope to take on staff and expand the business after the first year.

- After a year my expected turnover will put the business close to the VAT registration threshold. If the business is to expand further, I will have to register. Most of my customers will not be registered and will not be able to recover the VAT that they pay. This will equate to a significant price rise for them. My main competitor is VAT registered.

- My main competitor (which is a national franchise) is currently inefficient and not well-respected. However, it might improve its performance (possibly the franchise might be replaced) and offer more challenging competition.

- The other national franchise might open up in my area and provide strong competition.

Break-even

It is useful to know the amount of sales that must be made in order for the business to break-even. In order to make the calculation you need to know three things: A. The sales price per unit B. The amount of variable costs per unit C. The amount of fixed costs. The margin per unit is A minus B. The sales price per unit could relate to the goods that you sell or, for example, how much you charge for an hour of your services. The amount of variable costs per unit is the amount that varies according to the number of sales that you make. If you made no sales at all it would be NIL. The amount of fixed costs is the amount of expenditure that will be paid regardless of the volume of sales. It would not reduce even if no sales at all were made. The formula for calculating the amount of sales required to break-even is:

$$\frac{\textbf{Fixed costs}}{\textbf{Margin Per Unit}} \times \textbf{Sales price per unit}$$

This is best illustrated with an example. Valerie Smith imports and sells high quality leather wallets. She pays £120 per wallet and her other variable costs are £40 per wallet, making the total variable cost per wallet sold £160. She sells each wallet for £200, so the margin per wallet is £40. Her fixed costs are £40,000. The calculation is:

$$\frac{\textbf{£40,000}}{\textbf{£40}} = \textbf{1,000 wallets}$$

She must sell 1,000 wallets at £200 each, which will generate revenue of £200,000. This is the same as the costs which are as follows:

1,000 x £20 (to purchase wallets)	£120,000
1,000 x £40 (other variable costs)	£40,000
Fixed costs	£40,000
Total costs	**£200,000**

If she sells 1,001 wallets instead of 1,000 she will make a profit of £40, and if she only sells 999 she will make a loss of £40.

In practice it is almost never as clear cut as this, and for a number of reasons. The sales may be for a mixture of products and services, and the mix may vary from month to month. Discounts and other price variations may be introduced. Some costs are really semi-variable and expansion beyond a certain point may necessitate an increase in the fixed costs, taking extra premises for example. Despite all this the break-even calculation can be applied to the assumptions made in a plan or budget.

The break-even calculation is sometimes made as part of the business plan, though often it is not. It is obviously useful and highly motivating to know, even if not with complete accuracy, the level of business that must be achieved to cover your costs and start making a profit. Our personal experiences

During many years working in finance for companies I prepared numerous business plans and budgets. In my last few years as a financial director I started in a small way, as a sideline business on a self-employed basis, to deliver seminars and write books. When I began doing it full-time my business was already operating. I did not need to borrow money and I did not prepare a formal business plan as described in this chapter. I did, though, write down the key figures and satisfy myself that my plans were viable.

Chapter 6

Funding the business

It is a feature of nearly all business start-ups that money goes out before money comes in. Hopefully, of course, in time more money will come in than goes out and a profit will be made. It follows that nearly all new businesses will need some initial funding. In some of them the need will be small, but nevertheless something will be required. It is important, and the absence of suitable funding may frustrate your business plans. This is why the whole of this chapter is devoted to funding the business.

In many cases your own resources will be sufficient, perhaps supplemented by the help of family and friends. Furthermore, if you need a bank loan, the bank is likely to be distinctly unimpressed if you cannot or will not put something in yourself. Banks are of course the main source of finance other than yourself and your family and friends. These three sources are studied first in this chapter, but other possibilities are reviewed too. The list is:

- Your own savings and assets

- Family and friends

- Bank

- The Prince's Trust

- PRIME

- Royal British Legion

- Your pension fund

- Mortgages

- Asset financing

- Factoring and invoice discounting

- Grants

- Funding Circle

Your own savings and assets

These could perhaps add up to a worthwhile sum. Even if they are not sufficient to cover the complete requirement they could reduce the need to borrow from a bank or other source, and also make it easier to do so. You will know your own financial position, but the possibilities include shares, ISAs, premium bonds and other investments, and it might be possible to borrow against the surrender value of an endowment policy, if you have one. If you are leaving employment with a redundancy payment or some sort of pay off, this sum too might be available.

Could you manage with a less expensive car and are there possessions that could be sold? Such things as antiques, stamp collections and jewellery come to mind. You might be pleasantly surprised if you thought about it, and you might also realise that you have under-insured your possessions. I am the proud owner of a very unusual teapot which was once owned by Dame Nellie Melba. She gave it to her dresser and it passed through three other owners before it was given to me. I had it valued at £300 twenty years ago, but was told that if I could prove the link to Dame Nellie, which I cannot, its value would be tripled. This is an example of the sort of thing that I mean.

I know that to some people these suggestions may seem unrealistic or even impertinent, but there may be opportunities for others.

Family and friends

Family and friends are a common source of finance, and they quite often provide it interest free or at a low rate of interest. There are obvious advantages, but a possible unfortunate consequence is that relationships can suffer if the business fails, interest and repayments are made late or not at all, or if the lender believes that the borrower is acting unwisely or not trying hard enough. These problems can and do occur, and you may know of such cases.

If you are going down this route, it is important that you are very frank, tell the person concerned everything that they need to know and do not put an optimistic gloss on your plans. Verbal agreements are asking for trouble and the terms of a loan should be recorded in writing, probably prepared by a solicitor. This avoids uncertainty for the benefit of both parties, and the agreement should set out such things as the amount of the loan, interest, conditions and repayment dates.

A loan may be to a sole trader, a limited company, or a partnership and normally does not give any right to take a share of the profits or participate in running the business. If the family member or friend buys shares in a limited company, he or she will have the rights accorded to a shareholder. Another possibility is for the person to be a sleeping partner in a partnership. A further one is that the family member or friend might provide a guarantee for a bank loan.

Bank

All the major banks are willing to provide financial support for new and young businesses. This is with the qualification that the business must present a realistic proposal, that (in most cases) there must be personal guarantees and/or security, and that the bank must believe that there is a good chance of getting its money back. The last chapter advised on the preparation of a good business plan and a proposal prepared in this way is likely to be favourably reviewed, so long as the figures, guarantees and perhaps security are acceptable of course. According to a Business Manager at one of the major banks, the great majority of proposals that he receives are nowhere near this standard.

You will probably be aware that the banks have been much criticised since the credit crunch for their low amount of lending to small businesses. The banks respond by saying that the criticism is unfair and that they do have money to lend. All that they need are good proposals from small businesses, and that they have not received enough of them. Nevertheless, banks are heavily criticised and you may have your own views on the subject. Perhaps some of the bad feeling is caused by the common belief that the current economic difficulties have, partly at least, been caused by the banks and that many senior bankers are grossly overpaid. I must say, though, that the people in my own bank are very helpful and probably not overpaid.

All the major banks claim to support new businesses. Your record, character and credit history will be factors as well as the quality of your plan. If you have a good record with a personal account with the bank, it is a very good start. The same business manager mentioned earlier told me that his bank charges new small businesses no fee for arranging a loan up to £25,000, and that there would be a fixed APR of 9.4 per cent for a loan up to £15,000. This is of course at the time of writing and will not necessarily be the case in the future.

If you are self-employed, you have full personal liability for the debts of the business and this includes bank borrowing. If the business is a general partnership, each partner has full joint and several liability. This means that each partner can be made to pay 100 per cent of the partnership debts. This is recoverable pro rata from the other part- ners, but if they cannot pay or cannot be made to pay, the partner who can pay will be left paying the lot. This is worth very serious con- sideration if you are such a partner.

In the absence of misconduct the directors of a limited company do not have personal liability for the debts, and the liability of the share- holders is limited to the amount of the share capital. Of course the director or directors and the shareholder or shareholders are fre- quently the same person or persons. If you are borrowing on behalf of a limited company, the bank is very likely to ask for personal guaran- tees and, if the borrowing is substantial, some security such as a second charge on your house. I do strongly recommend that you dis- cuss this with your family, if relevant, before such a commitment is made.

A loan will be for a fixed term, at a fixed rate of interest and with repayments at fixed dates. The bank cannot demand early repayment or vary the terms unless the conditions of the loan are breached. An overdraft, on the other hand, is repayable on demand and the bank can vary the terms. Having said that, the bank is unlikely to demand repayment without notice and good reason, but it can. There are therefore benefits in taking a loan rather than an overdraft.

An Enterprise Finance Guarantee Loan is intended to provide help where there is a viable business plan, but the lender is unable to provide finance because sufficient security cannot be provided. It is a joint venture between participating lenders and the Department for Business Innovation and Skills (BIS). All the main banks are participating lenders. It must be stressed that it may be relevant only if there is a good business plan on which a bank (or other participating lender) is willing to lend. It is not intended to bolster up less than adequate proposals.

An Enterprise Finance Guarantee Loan is for small businesses up to five years old, and the repayment period may be up to a maximum of ten years. The Government takes a two percent premium on the outstanding balance of the loan, and for this it secures 75 per cent of the loan.

The bank or other lender still takes some risk. If your proposal for a loan is turned down because of insufficient security, it is something that may be worth discussing with your bank. Further information may be obtained from www.bis.gov.uk/efg.

I conclude with a final piece of advice. Do not ask the bank for less than you are going to need. It may be difficult to go back later and ask for more.

The Prince's Trust

This is a charity founded by the Prince of Wales and it gives support to unemployed and under-employed young people up to the age of 30. The amounts available are relatively small, but the Trust has successfully helped many young people. Low interest loans, grants and practical advice and support may be available. Of course it is not a soft touch – you have to have a worthwhile proposal. A good starting place is its website www.princes-trust.org.uk.

PRIME

This is a registered charity that helps people over 50 set up in business. Its website is www.primeinitiative.org.uk.

Royal British Legion

This charity exists to help men and women who have served in the armed forces. If this applies to you, it may be able to help. In particular, small interest-free, business loans may be available to unemployed ex-service men and women.

Your pension fund

It does not apply to the state pension, but if you are 55 or older you can take any private pension that you have and 25 per cent of the value can be taken as a tax free lump sum. The remainder would normally be taken at once as an annuity, but if the amount left is somewhat more than £30,000 it can probably be left to grow in a drawdown arrangement and not be taken immediately. This means that if you have a pension pot of say £60,000, a tax free lump sum of £15,000 can be accessed.

This information is provided with very significant reservations. Pensions are intended to provide a pension and security in one's latter years. If it is taken early, the amount is likely to be less and, according to your age at the time, perhaps very much less. Very careful thought is necessary before this step is taken and suitable advice should be sought.

Mortgages

A commercial mortgage is used to buy property for the business and the lender will take a legal charge over the premises as security. It will usually be a long term arrangement, with conditions and probably a not onerous rate of interest. The lender will undoubtedly expect an adequate margin of safety between the value of the property and the amount of the loan.

Asset financing

This is hire purchase or leasing and may be suitable if you acquire capital assets, such as cars, machinery etc.

In the case of hire purchase you pay for the asset over a period and the asset becomes your property when payment has been made in full. The interest element of the instalments is a charge to the profit and loss account. The capital cost is subject to depreciation in the profit and loss account. In the case of leasing you have the use of the asset without owning it. The payments to the leasing company are a charge in the profit and loss account.

If you refer back to the example of a business plan in the last chapter, you will see that the capital items in set-up costs may well have been suitable for hire purchase or leasing. It would have made a big difference to the initial funding required, though of course payments would have been required during the first few years.

Factoring and invoice discounting

The main attraction of factoring is that the factoring company gives you up to about 75 per cent of the amount invoiced to customers, and does so within a very few days of the invoice being issued. The customer pays the factoring company and you then get the remainder. So if you ask for payment in 60 days and the customer actually takes 75 days, you will get 75 per cent of the money about 70 days earlier than would otherwise be the case. Of course, the factor deducts a fee and interest. Sometimes the factor takes the bad debt risk and sometimes not. Factoring may be available for business to business sales, but it will not be an option if you sell to the public.

Invoice discounting is similar but a proportion of the total amount of the debts outstanding is advanced, rather than the advance being related to a specific invoice. Factoring and invoice discounting come at a cost, but it is less than is often supposed.

Factoring and invoice discounting do not help with the start-up costs of a business, but it is a common and effective way of improving the cash flow when you are up and running. The factoring company is very likely to want you to be established before it deals with you. A good place to start is the website of The Asset Based Finance Association which is www.abfa.org.uk.

Grants

There are many hundreds or even thousands of possibilities for grants and you may be eligible for one or more. Among numerous other sources, grants may be available from or via the European Union, Central Government, Local Government, Development Agencies and Chambers of Commerce.

Good places to start are your local Enterprise Agency and Business Link. The latter is particularly good and you might like to look at their website www.businesslink.gov.uk. There are so many possible grants that it would be futile to try and list them all here. Do not be afraid to make enquiries. Some grants may be to provide finance and others may be for such things as training.

Unfortunately applying for a grant may be a rather bureaucratic process and there may be a significant delay whilst it is considered. Another point to consider is that some grants have the purpose of persuading you to do something that you would not otherwise do, and this could perhaps be seen as a negative factor. If, for example, the grant is in return for you employing a particular type of person in Scunthorpe and you would otherwise employ a different type of person somewhere else, the implications should be considered very carefully. The best grants, from your point of view, are for doing something that you planned to do anyway.

Funding Circle

This links businesses with potential backers. Apart from possibly providing funding it has the benefit of seeing if a proposal stands up to scrutiny. It can be checked out on www.fundingcircle.com/business. The website summarises its purpose as follows:

> 'Funding Circle is an online marketplace where real people lend to UK businesses where businesses get fast access to finance to continue growing their business, and people get better returns on their money. By cutting out the high costs and complexity of banks both sides are better off.'

Chapter 7

Finding your customers

The need to find customers is something that will worry quite a few people considering self-employment and it will be a very big concern for some. In fact, they may wonder if they can do it. Many people come to self-employment from an environment where finding customers is not a problem or it is done by other people. This is particularly true of the public sector. For example, finding customers is hardly a problem for employees of HMRC. It is obviously extremely important because without customers you have not got a business. No matter how good the idea and the organisation, it will not succeed without customers.

This chapter examines the main ways in which customers are found, some of them overlapping, but the list is not exhaustive and there are other creative possibilities. For example I recently saw a roundabout in Wolverton that was sponsored by a local fish bar and an enticing notice said that it was only 200 yards away. I made a mental note to check it out the next time that I am passing. Sponsorship of local events and good causes may be something else worth considering.

It is sometimes said that the best things in life are free and it can be true in business too. A letter to a newspaper costs next to nothing and can subtly mention the name of your business. Of course the letter must be interesting and worthy of publication. Best of all is getting something included as editorial. It is much more likely than an advert-isement to be seen and trusted.

Every time that a customer or other business contact sees your sta-tionery a subtle message is conveyed. Not everyone would agree, but in my view this is not an area where you should economise. Letters, compliments slips, business cards, invoices, statements and other stationery should tell everyone that this is a substantial business that takes itself seriously and is here to stay.

This chapter will hopefully inspire a positive attitude and a resolve to get going and find customers, all of which is splendid, but do not get carried away. It is not uncommon for too much money to be spent. All the expenditure should be justified and affordable. In particular it is possible to spend a fortune on advertising campaigns and to regret it afterwards. It is probably desirable to try a limited campaign first and then move on to something bigger if the results justify it.

The following topics are covered in this chapter:

- Your existing contacts and old employer

- Website

- Social networking

- Leaflets, paper mailshots and electronic mailshots

- Advertising

- Networking

- Word of mouth

- Shows and exhibitions

- Shop windows

- Our personal experiences

In conclusion – please do not neglect your existing customers. This is obviously not relevant as soon as you start, but it is afterwards. Once you have started trading it is important that you retain your customers. This is of course said with the proviso that it is a customer that you want to retain – not a potential bad debt and possibly not a slow payer either. As a general rule it costs quite a lot more to find a new customer than it does to retain an existing one. A dissatisfied customer is not just a potential loss of future business, it is a source of negative publicity that may counteract the positive things that you are doing to attract new business.

Your existing contacts and old employer

The relevance of this will depend on what you will be doing and how closely it relates to your previous employment. If you intend to be an electrician on the Isle of Skye, your experience as an IT consultant in Swansea will not be much help. On the other hand, for quite a few people, existing contacts and their old employer can be the springboard for a successful launch into self-employment.

In some cases your family and friends may help you get your business going. They may be in a position to give you some early orders and at the least will help spread the word. This is so well recognised that some employers train new sales staff to do it, the financial services sector being an obvious example. Before moving on it is perhaps worth dwelling on the old saying that you should be careful about mixing business with pleasure. It is possible that family and friends may resent being approached or used as they may see it, and you will certainly want to make sure that they are not disappointed with the goods and services that you provide.

Chapter 2 is about leaving your present employer. It could be very relevant here and it might be a good idea to look at it again. The advice is not repeated, but for some their old employer may be their launchpad for future success. Your old friends and colleagues may be of some help and may be future customers. Needless to say, you should only do what is legally and morally acceptable.

Of course your business contacts may not necessarily be restricted to your old employer. You may have friends and contacts from a number of jobs. They too may be useful, especially if you will be in the same line of business. Some people make an effort to maintain contact details as their careers develop and they progress through life. I did not do it myself but it is an idea with much to commend it. If this is not something that you have done, it is a bit late to start now, but you may be able to look up some old friends.

Website

Perhaps your business will not benefit from having a website, but it is quite likely that it will and it is certainly something that should be considered. The number of business websites increases sharply year by year and you may risk losing sales and opportunities if you do not keep up. Chapter 5 contains a completely fictitious business plan for an imaginary person planning to set up a company that will maintain lawns in the Aylesbury area. To test my observations on websites I did a google search for the words 'Lawn care Aylesbury'. This produced the incredible total of 37,400 entries, which is of course the weakness of a google search. It is all too easy to drown in too much information. After stripping out sundry care homes and such things as florists one is left with useful entries for enterprises such as gardeners and fertiliser suppliers. Then near the top are several businesses that maintain lawns in the way described in Chapter 5. Clearly this is not something that my fictitious budding entrepreneur should ignore.

Having said that, it is not always necessary or appropriate and it costs time and money to set up. So the first question is whether or not to have a website. Assuming that the answer is 'yes' the next decision is whether it will just provide information about the business, its products and services, or whether it will go further and cater for online ordering and payment. If it does this, the website will be more expensive to design, install and maintain.

Your website, if you have one, should be at least moderately good and preferably very good. A poor one will not impress potential customers and, at worst, it may actually deter them. You will not achieve the required standard without investing some time and money. The next decision is whether you will do it yourself or pay someone to do it. Many people have the necessary skills to create at least an adequate website. If this includes you and if you have the time and the inclination, it probably makes sense to do it yourself. If not, you should get some help. There are a lot of good website designers around, as well as some bad ones of course.

Setting up and running a website is a very big subject but the following hints should help get good results:

1. If you use a website designer, do not lose control of the project. You should 'own' it and the end result should be what you want,

not what someone else wants. Keep in close touch with your designer throughout the project. This is not a criticism of website designers, most of whom would endorse this advice.

2. Your website should not be crowded and it should be easy to use. Potential customers will be irritated if this is not the case. It is very easy to click on to a website but it is very easy to click away as well. Most website visits are of short duration. There should be an attractive front page and logically laid out supporting pages.

3. Your website should include your name and contact details. If your business is a registered company, it is a legal requirement that it include certain statutory details. These are the company's registered name, registered number, place of registration and registered office. These details can be available via a link from the front page. It is probably a good idea for your trading terms and conditions to be similarly available.

4. Pay attention to security and anti-virus software.

5. Customers and potential customers should know about your website. The world's best website is of limited value if not many people use it. It is a good idea to mention your website on your business stationery.

6. Your website will need a suitable hosting company and a carefully chosen domain name. There is a lot to be said for incorporating in it a description of what you do. For example www.rogermason-businessbooks.com is probably better than www.rogermason.com, or it could be something like www.quality-businessbooks.com. When the time comes do not forget to renew the domain name. If you do forget, it will become available and

someone else may exploit the goodwill in it. At the very least, people may be confused.

7. It is important that the website is maintained and kept up to date. Few things are more annoying than out of date information.

8. If you trade online, as opposed to just providing information, you will have to make arrangements to accept payments. You will need to register with a service such as PayPal.

Before leaving websites it is worth revisiting the subject of internet search engines such as Google, because there are obvious advantages in appearing near the top of the list for relevant searches. I present seminars for a company called UK Training and some of my colleagues specialise in VAT training. If you use Google and enter the words 'VAT Training' you will find that UK Training is listed almost at the beginning of a very long list of entries. This did not happen by accident. It may well be worth trying to get your website into this desirable position. If you do not have the skills necessary to accomplish this, it will be necessary to employ suitable help.

If you conduct a search on Google or Yahoo you will see a number of advertisements appearing close to the information you are checking. They may well irritate you because you may think that they are not relevant and you do not wish to see them. Nevertheless, you are still exposed to them. It is rather like choosing to watch a TV programme on a commercial channel and accepting the adverts as a consequence of doing so. These adverts have been placed on a pay-per-click basis and the advert placers pay a charge to the website owner every time someone clicks on to them. It is something that you might consider.

Social networking

One of the most significant developments in recent times regarding the Internet has been the growth of Social Networking sites. As with many developments in technology, many pretenders have come and gone but the most significant players remaining in the field are probably Facebook, Twitter and LinkedIn. These three sites, still in their infancy, have a combined market value of £56 billion.

There are many practical advantages from which a business may benefit by investing time and perhaps money in social networking. Networking is the important word to remember. If your business benefits from ordinary networking then the Internet provides an excellent opportunity to amplify these efforts and network with many more people.

I would list the following as being particular advantages to a business trying to find customers using social networking tools:

- Building, developing and cementing relationships with clients. Relationships are crucial to winning future business from existing customers.

- Cultivating a sense of 'celebrity' or 'notoriety' for your company. Helping to get your name known and perhaps generate additional publicity from conventional media sources.

- Reinforcing 'branding' – getting your company logo widely seen and recognised.

- Apart from the investment of time, using social networks is free or low-cost.

- Once you are connected with people, it is a no-cost form of communicating with a group of people interested in your services.

- Topicality, immediacy and speed of response

- Increasing accessibility, especially with the increased use of iPhones, android phones and iPads.

However, there are also potential difficulties of which you should beware. The old saying that there is 'no fool like a busy fool' could well have been coined for the Internet age. Social networking can be massively distracting and you could well spend many happy hours making lots of friends and not a single penny. It is important to have a strategic view and a sense of discipline.

Another danger which is particular to the Internet is the existence of Trolls and as any billy goat can tell you - Trolls mean trouble! A Troll is someone who causes disruption, often in an inflammatory or offensive way, by posting things in response to the posts of others. In some recent cases involving Facebook and Twitter, these activities have escalated to such a degree that charges of harassment have been brought by the police. Falling foul of people who are disparaging about you or your business on the Internet can not only be upsetting but also potentially ruinous to your reputation. Unfortunately, bad news can often go viral faster than good news.

One final note of caution should be to make sure that if you raise expectations, you are able to meet them. Many businesses introduce themselves on social networks using offers and coupons to draw in new customers. If you do so, then make sure you limit your offer to what you are able to deliver. Vouchers can be re-circulated online in an instant and a loss-leader can quickly turn into a total loss! Rachel Brown, who owns a cupcake bakery in Berkshire, offered a 75 per cent discount on her products via a well-known coupon site, expecting a few hundred responses. She received 8,500 responses making a loss of between £2.50 and £3.00 in each order as well as having to pay £12,500 in additional production costs. Obviously, her profits for the year were wiped out.

Facebook

The key word with regard to social networking using Facebook is 'social'. Many users regard Facebook as a personal, almost private, space on the Internet where they can share thoughts and feelings with friends and family. The intrusion of overt advertising could therefore arouse resentment in some and you can soon find yourself 'unliked' and hidden from view. However, Facebook does offer a Pay Per Click service which is not dissimilar to Google's Adwords service. The adverts can be intelligently targeted to be seen by users who have 'liked' the kind of things that you are offering.

The real strength of Facebook though is in setting up a business page which enables you to develop the relationship with your customers. You can turn customers into 'friends' and engage in a dialogue that can involve many people. You can use photos and videos to explain and promote your wares, and you can invite people to leave comments about their positive experiences and recommend your services to their friends. Many companies also use their Facebook pages for specific promotions, product launches or invitations to events.

It is important to interact and engage, ignoring contact from your customers online is as bad as ignoring them when they walk into your shop!

Twitter

Twitter is a service where users write posts of 140 characters or less called tweets. You can see what people tweet by 'following' them. Whereas Facebook is mostly about communicating with friends and family, Twitter is mostly about following and communicating with people or organisations that have something to say in which you are interested. Celebrities such as Stephen Fry or, globally, Lady Gaga are among the most followed on Twitter. There are many key figures in business who also have many thousands of people hanging on their every tweet.

The essential attraction of Twitter over some other forms of social networking is in its brevity and its immediacy. Many important items of news are first spread on Twitter before reaching mainstream media outlets. This makes Twitter very topical and fast moving. If you can take advantage of this in promoting your services then it may be of use. However, the immediacy of Twitter can also translate into transience – a carefully composed tweet can be lost in a sea of others. Better to tweet regularly or plan a series of tweets as part of a campaign.

In order to make the most of Twitter you will need to build up a significant list of followers. You can do this by promoting your Twitter account in your general promotions and stationery, making exclusive offers to followers and by ensuring that your tweets are relevant, topical and preferably amusing. This encourages people to 're-tweet' your posts and recommend their followers to follow you. Twitter displays a real-time list of 'trending' topics and engaging in these discussions can also increase your profile and notoriety.

LinkedIn

LinkedIn is social networking for professionals and business people. If your business is in selling to other businesses then LinkedIn has a lot to recommend it. It allows you to 'connect' with other professionals and organisations with whom you may share an interest. There is also the opportunity to advertise on the site on a pay-per-click basis.

It is possible to promote your business by posting announcements or offers in ways similarly to those previously discussed, however the real strength of LinkedIn is in the opportunity to build networks. Satisfied clients can use LinkedIn to 'Recommend' you, with some LinkedIn users having hundreds of recommendations. This can be powerful, if virtual, word of mouth advertising.

Another powerful aspect of LinkedIn is the use of Groups and Bulletin Boards. These tools are ostensibly for sharing knowledge and information, tips and hints. Indeed, should you have a particular query to which you cannot otherwise find an answer then posting it on a board on LinkedIn is an excellent option. But there is also the opportunity to sell your services to other businesses in a particular sector, such as Human Resources.

Unlike some other social networking sites, LinkedIn limits some of its services for free users and you will have to pay a subscription fee to take advantage of the full range of services.

There can be many and munificent benefits for those businesses for whom it is important to develop long-lasting relationships. Patience is the perhaps the most significant investment. It takes time, certainly more than a few months, to establish a network of meaningful quality, which in this context is always more important than quantity.

There are marketing professionals and agencies who, for a fee, will manage your social networking campaigns for you. If you think that this type of relationship can bring a significant financial boost to your enterprise then it may well be an investment worth considering.

Leaflets, paper mailshots and electronic mailshots

It is very desirable that your advertising targets your potential market rather than the world at large, cost of course being the main reason. One of the advantages of leaflets and mailshots is that it should be possible to aim them in this way.

Leaflets can, with considerable expense, be distributed with a scatter-gun approach over a large area. Alternatively they can with some care be directed towards likely clients. For example your monthly Saga magazine, if you subscribe to it, will come with an assortment of leaflets in the package. Many of them will have the over 50s, who comprise most of the readership, very much in mind. You will see pictures of ecstatically happy senior citizens doing such things as using stairlifts, hearing aids and walk-in showers. It is presumably an effective way of selling these products.

Your leaflets can be put through letterboxes individually by hand. If you are targeting a very local area, this is something that you could do yourself and distribution does not come cheaper than that. There are various alternatives including paying people to do it or arranging to have them delivered with newspapers. If your leaflet comes through the letterbox individually, it is perhaps more likely to be read.

The handful of leaflets that come with the Saga magazine may be swiftly discarded.

I know that local leaflets can work because I have purchased the services that they publicise. A recent example was a first-class leaflet offering to clear out my gutters for £75. I telephoned the number given and within a minute a very helpful woman had located my house on Google Earth and confirmed that the high gutters and one over a conservatory would not be a problem. A few days later her husband did a very good job indeed.

Direct mail is in some ways rather like leaflets and, indeed, may include leaflets. An individually addressed letter is more likely to engage the attention of the recipient, though it is of course more expensive. I am part of the minority that thinks that Royal Mail generally does quite a good job, but postage on top of the other costs is a very significant factor. Royal Mail can take quite a long time to deliver 'junk mail' but that probably does not matter. A cheaper variation of direct mail in paper form is direct marketing in electronic form. This will probably not cost as much but the failure rate will probably be higher, though not everyone would agree with this observation.

Once you have been in business for a considerable time you probably can, and should, accumulate valuable data about your customers and other suitable recipients of your mailshots and leaflets, but of course this will not help you in the early days. You may be able to work something out for yourself but you will probably need to talk to a list broker. These businesses supply, for a charge that may be quite considerable, targeted mail and electronic lists for your use. They may classify the lists by such things as:

- Size of business

- Geographic area

- Income range

- Age

- Interests, hobbies etc

When considering leaflets and mailshots please keep three important points in mind:

1. The take-up response is likely to be very low. Circumstances vary but many businesses consider that a one per cent response is a good result.

2. As with all forms of publicity it is worth taking some care. Good quality paper and printing are probably a worthwhile investment. Silly mistakes with grammar and spelling are definitely to be avoided.

3. Some people try to protect themselves from what they consider to be 'junk mail' but what you might consider to be 'a valuable purchasing opportunity'. They do this by signing up for the Mail Preference Service (MPS). It would be at least unsporting and probably counter-productive to disregard this. It might also get you into legal difficulties. The same applies to the Telephone Preference Service (TPS). Your list broker should protect you by not supplying lists containing forbidden contacts. It is worth checking.

Advertising

Advertising can be extremely effective but it is possible to spend a lot of money without being certain of the results. At one time Unilever spent more money on advertising than any other British company. Lord Leverhulme, who put the company together, once said that he knew that half of his advertising expenditure was wasted. He went on to say that he did not know which half.

An early decision must be made. This is whether to make advertising widescale or even national, or specialised and local. Unilever takes the former course on the grounds that the market for soap powder is much the same in Manchester as in Plymouth. This is the expensive option, though economies of scale will be available. The other option is to make the advertising specialised and/or local. It is very likely that almost all readers will sensibly choose the second option. This will be much cheaper and it will make it important that the advertising is very carefully targeted at the right people.

The A.I.D.A. formula is often quoted in advertising circles. It translates as:

- **Attention** - The advert, probably by means of a headline, must get the attention of the reader. Unless the reader's attention is engaged the advert is a failure.

- **Interest** - The reader should be sufficiently interested to give the advert some time, perhaps just a very little time.

- **Desire** - The reader should want to have whatever is being advertised.

- **Action** - The advert should invite the reader to fulfil the desire by making a purchase. It should say how this should be done – by providing a contact telephone number for example.

It is not a bad formula to follow and if you can do all that you should make sales. Do not underestimate the importance of the first A.

Unless your advert gets attention it is a failure right from the start.

If you are placing a not very large text-only advert in a local paper, you can probably compose it all yourself. Do take care, remember A.I.D.A., and give it a compelling heading. If you are doing something ambitious, it may be sensible to get professional help with the design. It is a good idea to study the papers or magazines in which you will advertise, look at the adverts and copy the best ideas and layout. Imitation is the sincerest form of flattery. Do not make the advert too detailed or complicated. This is a common mistake.

There are advantages in a series of repeated adverts. Readers may pass over the first one but eventually, and perhaps subconsciously think that it is familiar and worth a look. This is particularly true for something new. It is not the case that familiarity breeds contempt.

In conclusion it is worth returning to the need to target the advertising carefully and this is very well illustrated by the experience of a friend who started a business. It included training people for a role that included some public speaking. He thought that it would appeal to a range of people with suitable experience such as toastmasters, retired school teachers and people who were used to taking an active part in church meetings. With this in mind he placed small adverts in the Business Opportunities sections of the Daily Mail and Daily Express. The adverts cost several thousands of pounds and had the potential to be seen by millions of people. Despite this the response was almost non-existent. He then advertised in church magazines with a circulation of just thousands. The adverts cost less than £50 each and he got a good response.

Networking

The first aim of networking is to try and ensure that many people know what you do and that you do it well. The second aim is to try and see that as many of them as possible are the right people. The right people are of course your potential customers. To use a popular but rather vulgar phrase you must put yourself about a bit. This is second nature to some people but will not come easily to many. It is, though, important.

A friend who was for many years employed in the financial services industry has told me that recruits were told to put themselves into what were called 'centres of influence'. These could be organisations such as sports clubs and charitable organisations. You may already be active in such organisations, but if not perhaps you should make the effort to be so. There are obvious advantages in selecting centres of influence whose aims you share and whose activities you will enjoy. Make friends and talk to people. A hard sell would almost certainly not be appropriate and would probably be resented, but it should not be hard to let people know what you do. Hopefully they will like you, respect you and think that you probably do a good job.

It sounds cynical and indeed perhaps it is cynical, but it may well work and, if you select the organisation wisely, you will get the benefit of enjoying the club and the activity. For example, if it is a sports club it should help you keep fit. Being self-employed may be lonely and this sort of networking can help alleviate this problem. Other possibilities include Chambers of Commerce, Trade Associations and Business Clubs. My home town has a Business Breakfast Club that meets regularly at 7.30 am.

Do favours for people. As well as being good for the soul this has the advantage that favours may later be returned. The world does sometimes work in this way. Except when you are in your pyjamas always carry some business cards and do not mind leaving them. They should be good quality cards. Anything else is a false economy.

Word of mouth

Let's start with something very obvious and very important. If you provide value for money and a good service, word will get around. This will be the case even if you do little or nothing to speed along the process, but of course you should try to do just that. I am sure that you can think of personal experiences to back this up. Just this week two friends have said that they will visit the theatre and see a play that I have recommended to them. One of them had not even heard of the play. That's the power of word of mouth.

It will probably not escape your notice that word of mouth works for negative experiences too. In fact experience of bad service is more likely to be passed on than news of good service. The moral is that there is no substitute for getting the product and service right.

You should always have a supply of good promotional material and business cards and give them to satisfied clients. A more aggressive approach may be resented and be counterproductive. Clients may well be willing to help in this way, especially for a new business. Do not forget to thank them and give them feedback if any business results from what they do. Furthermore, you should return the compliment and pass on the word for them.

Shows and exhibitions

It may well be prohibitively expensive to take a stand at a major national or international show or exhibition. So it is probably not suitable for a new small business. In the longer term though, who knows? More local and smaller shows are another matter and may be worth serious consideration.

Whether or not this is a good idea will depend on the show and the nature of the goods and services that you provide. If your business involves crafts, there will certainly be plenty of suitable opportunities. The advantages are the sales that you make on the day and the chance to promote your business to a receptive group. Make sure that your stand is well presented and that you have some good promotional material.

Shop windows

Placing cards in shop windows is just about the cheapest method of all, extremely local and for some types of business very effective. Have a look at some newsagents and other display areas. You will almost certainly see cards advertising local micro businesses. These are likely to include such things as slimming clubs, dog walkers, baby sitters and gardeners. It is not suitable for many businesses but it is for others. It's cheap and it works. We know that first hand because we are just about to book the services of a man whose card has the enticing title of 'MAN WITH A VAN'.

A study of these cards may well leave you feeling depressed about educational standards. Spelling and grammatical mistakes are all too common. Apart from anything else this is bad for business. You probably do not need the reminder, but take care.

Our personal experiences

In each of my final years of full-time employment, and in my own time, I presented a few seminars for different companies. In addition, and also in my own time, I wrote a number of books, some of them for Thorogood. Therefore, when my employment was terminated I was able to hit the ground running.

I approached a number of seminar companies and quickly reached an agreement to present a significant number of seminars for UK Training. I also continued presenting two seminars a year for ICSA. These arrangements continue to this day. Over the years I have been asked by publishers (including Thorogood) to write certain books. In addition, I took various proposals to publishers. Some of these proposals were accepted and some were not.

My wife was a part-time Deputy Registrar of Births, Marriages and Deaths when she decided to become a Civil Funeral Celebrant. She made a number of very well thought out presentations to local Funeral Directors. These were extremely well received and she was quickly given a lot of bookings. As a result she gave up her position as a Deputy Registrar.

We were both rapidly in the fortunate position of having all the work that we wanted. Both of our businesses are very personal to us and we each made the decision not to take on staff and not to expand beyond what we can do ourselves. Neither of us has a website and we have not followed most of the paths described in this chapter. However, the one that we do take very seriously is networking. We each have a small number of direct clients who make our services available to larger groups.

Chapter 8

Running the business

This book contains much advice about starting a business, so it does not come amiss to include a chapter about running it after you have got going. The following important topics are featured:

- Your computer

- Dealing with customer complaints

- Effective time management

- Bank account

- Managing cashflow

- Credit control

- Our personal experiences

Your computer

As you will know, the world of computers does not stand still. Hardware and particularly business software develop from year to year, in many cases operate more quickly from year to year and in some cases get cheaper from year to year. All this is good news because it should enable you to save time and work more effectively. You may not use a computer in running your business but it is likely that you will, and you may not own a computer before you start your business venture but it is likely that you will once you set up your business. Computers will probably play an important part in running your office and your business. It is a very big subject but this section of the chapter aims to give some useful pointers towards getting good results.

The following are among the numerous possible applications for your computer:

- Sending and receiving e-mails
- Word processing
- Spreadsheets – the many potential uses include the preparation of cashflow forecasts
- Keeping accounting records and preparing accounts
- Presentations
- Keeping records of customers and suppliers
- Skype, which is free at the moment, allows you to have face to face business discussions with customers or others. The other party must be signed up to it and give you their Skype address.
- Sage (website www.sage.co.uk) is generally recognised as the leading supplier of accounting packages and Microsoft is generally recognised as the market leader in business software. Microsoft's applications include:
  - Publisher – this is for desktop publishing.
  - PowerPoint – this is useful for making high quality audio visual displays. It is very beneficial in making presentations.

- Excel – this is a spreadsheet program that allows you to make calculations using a large quantity of data that can be easily manipulated. The preparation of budgets is an example of an application for which it is useful.
- Word – this is a comprehensive word processing program. It can also be used to create web pages.

You will need to decide whether to go for desktop, laptop or perhaps both. Desktop computers are designed for use in a fixed location. They are generally a little cheaper than laptops and by spending a little more you can get something more powerful, though you might not need the extra speed and capacity. A desktop computer will require a separate monitor, keyboard and mouse. The great advantage of laptops is their portability. They can be taken with you and used in a wide variety of locations, as can frequently be witnessed on trains and in cafes. They have an integrated monitor, keyboard and mouse. It is possible to have a docking station and then use the laptop as an ordinary computer.

You will need a printer and fortunately these have become progressively cheaper. In fact you can buy a reasonable one for about £30, though if you have special needs (a requirement for printing in colour or on A3 paper for example) greater expenditure may be needed. What has not got cheaper are the ink cartridges, which is where the manufacturers make their money. You will be urged to only use the manufacturer's cartridges which, if you are a big user, can cost you a lot of money. Other cartridges that claim to be compatible may be purchased for a fraction of the cost. These may be satisfactory, but they may cause problems. It is probably worth trying them out or perhaps using them alternately with the manufacturer's ones. You may well find that the cheaper the printer, the more expensive the manufacturer's cartridges will be.

Your software may check your grammar and feature a spellchecker. I advise you to treat these with caution. They may favour American spelling and may have problems with grammar. 'There/their' is likely to cause a problem. Ours rejects the biblical wording of the Lord's prayer and substitutes 'For thine are the kingdom' for 'For thine is the kingdom'.

Fortunately there are quite a lot of computer experts around operating as small businesses and some of them are very good. They are willing to act as trouble-shooters at short notice when something goes wrong. It is worth getting to know one, it might save you a lot of anxiety.

Before leaving the subject of computers please take a moment to absorb three golden rules.

- Viruses can cause havoc. Take virus protection seriously and update your anti-virus software regularly.

- Be disciplined with the computer and regularly delete out of date information stored on it.

- Do regular backups to avoid losing important information. The loss of key data may cause dreadful problems.

Dealing with customer complaints

A visitor to London stopped a passer by and asked the best way to Trafalgar Square. He received the reply 'If I was going to Trafalgar

Square, I wouldn't be starting from here'. It is a very old joke and the places and nationalities are interchangeable. For some reason Dublin and the Irish often feature, but as I am English and as I do not want to give offence I have adjusted it. The point of the story is that if you are in the right place to start with, you do not need to take corrective action. Get the product or service right and you will get few, if any, complaints. This is of course a counsel of perfection and some complaints are almost inevitable, but get the basics right and ensure that complaints are as few as possible.

How you deal with complaints is extremely important. Most customers do not remember or talk about most experiences. They do remember and talk about experiences that are particularly good or particularly bad. They may well remember favourably a bad experience that has been promptly and effectively put right. You will, like me, undoubtedly have many experiences that support this. My personal favourite concerns the Sunday Times Wine Club, from which I have bought wine for many years. They have a no quibble guarantee which says that if you do not enjoy a wine for any reason they will immediately replace it free of charge. I have only complained once and I did immediately receive a no quibble replacement. A few days later I remembered that I had bought the offending wine from someone else and, honest man that I am, I rang and told them. They laughed and said that I should keep the replacement bottle with their compliments.

Of course not all complaints are justified. An unjustified complaint may be a cynical move by an unscrupulous customer or, probably more likely, put in by a customer who has a different view to your own. If you believe that a complaint is unjustified, it is usually best to courteously give your reasons for rejecting it and regret that the customer believes that you have not met their expectations.

If the complaint is justified, you should quickly take steps to put things right. This may be a replacement article (as with the Sunday Times Wine Club) or remedial work. It may also be a credit or refund. Just possibly a goodwill gesture might be appropriate and appreciated. You should always take complaints seriously and, whatever you do or do not do, act quickly.

Putting something right may cost a lot but often does not do so. There may be scope for doing something that minimises your cost. For example, you might provide free servicing for which you would normally charge £200, but which costs you £100.

This section concludes with a final very important piece of advice. If you are wrong, SAY SORRY.

Effective time management

Many self-employed people fail to achieve a good work/life balance. This may be because they do not devote enough time to work, but it is much more likely to be because they give too much time and emotional commitment to work and not enough to their family, friends and interests. Furthermore, they may tend to talk too much about their work and try the patience of other people. This is a shame, particularly since a wish to have a good work/life balance may have been a reason for choosing self-employment in the first place.

You should try to organise your work so as to ensure that you have a reasonable amount of free time. Apart from anything else, if you do work too long and too hard, you may experience the law of diminishing returns and the quality of your work may suffer. This is of course not to deny that hard work is very important, but you should aim to work effectively as well as hard. It may not be easy, but the following tips are designed to help you get it right:

- It may be a good idea to pay people to do things that you are capable of doing yourself. This will be free time for you. You may choose to use it as 'me time' or you may use it for what is the main point of your business and what you do well. This is likely to maximise your profits. For example, if you are a computer programmer, you are likely to earn more from a morning programming computers than you will save by spending the morning stuffing envelopes for a mailshot.

- Once a day, or at least frequently, take just a few moments to write down a short list of outstanding jobs and put them in order of priority. Do not be unrealistic and depress yourself with an impossible list. Some people make this either their first or last job of the day.

- Keep your office, working environment and everything connected with your work tidy. This means such things as keeping the filing up to date. To borrow a well known phrase 'Don't put it down, put it away'. It may seem tedious but it will probably save time in the long run.

- Work in ways that mesh with your character and natural inclinations. To use a woodworking term, work with the grain. You will know if you are a natural early bird or a natural night owl. There is something to be said for doing the most demanding work when you are at your most alert. Routine jobs requiring not too much thought can perhaps be done at other times.

Bank account

Your bank as a source of start-up finance is covered in Chapter 6. This chapter is intended to help you choose and run your bank account most effectively, and to get the best possible deal from your bank. This is on an on-going basis, though of course the right foundations should be laid at the start.

To repeat a point made elsewhere, it is almost certainly a good idea to have a business bank account separate from your personal bank account. This may not, but probably will, be with the same bank. It will be a requirement if you have a company and virtually a requirement if you operate on a self-employed basis with a trading name. My bank is not allowed to credit a cheque payable to Roger Mason Limited to the personal bank account of Roger Mason, and this is true for all limited companies.

Regardless of the legal niceties, it helps you run your business in a disciplined way if you have separate bank accounts and separate book-keeping records. There is something to be said for separate credit cards and a few true believers even go as far as to have separate wallets or purses for their business cash. When it comes to self-discipline and separation of roles perhaps we have something to learn from the great Victorian prime minister William Gladstone. He was the one who, as you may know, always chewed his food 39 times before swallowing. This may or may not have been literally true, but he certainly had three separate desks in his home. One was for government business, one was for Party business and one was for his personal and family affairs.

I should though mention a possible benefit of using your personal bank account for business purposes if you are self-employed and trade in just your own name. You probably do not pay bank charges on your personal bank account, whereas, perhaps after an initial period, you probably will on a business account. The bank most definitely will not like this practice, but it might not find out. It would know if you borrow money, pay in cash to the bank or have a significantly higher number of transactions. A possible reason for using a personal credit card for business expenses is that you will get the points or whatever inducement the card company offers. You can reimburse yourself for the business-related entries on the statements with monthly cheques. This is not a bad idea, but self-discipline is absolutely essential.

You might be one of the very small number of people who believe that banks never make mistakes and that checking is therefore unnecessary. If so, please disabuse yourself of this mistaken belief. Banks have always made mistakes and certainly I made some a long time ago when I worked for the Midland Bank. They still do. The difference is that they are now more likely to be computerised mistakes, though of course computers only make mistakes that have been entered or programmed into them by fallible humans. Not only do fallible banks make mistakes, fallible business men and women do too. So in checking on your bank, you are checking on yourself as well.

Get regular bank statements, at least monthly and perhaps more often. This may not happen automatically, so you might have to ask. Then promptly and systematically reconcile the statements with your own records. This will be easier and can be done at any time if you are one of the growing number of people who use online banking.

Advice on doing this is given in Chapter 9. Follow up any discrepancies and charges that you think may be incorrect. They will very probably have been caused by you, but take them up with the bank if necessary.

Many years ago people and businesses often felt a very strong loyalty to a particular bank and this was reciprocated by the bank, but even in the good old days of the fictional Captain Mainwaring and Dad's Army banks existed primarily to make profits for their owners. They were good at it too. Today the focus on making profits is more pronounced and perhaps mutual loyalty is less appropriate. There is nothing wrong with banks trying to maximise their profits and it is what you will be doing with your own business, but you are entitled to treat them in the same way as other suppliers. In a nutshell:

- Choose the best deal

- Hold them to it

- Watch the charges

- Say no to unwanted extras that come with charges

- Remember that you may be able to get some of the extras, insurance for example, cheaper elsewhere

- Remember that you have the right, if you can, to take your business elsewhere

The other side of the coin is that the bank is entitled to expect you to play fair and tell the truth. In the interests of both you and the bank, you should volunteer information and try to develop a good relationship.

It can take a while to set up a new business bank account so, if possible, approach the bank and put in hand the arrangements in plenty of time. All the banks have special deals for new businesses, so talk to them and try to make sure that you get the one that is best for you. Some accounts may give you an initial period free of bank charges. Others may allow you to operate permanently free of bank charges, though almost certainly this will be subject to conditions. The most likely condition is that at least a certain minimum sum be credited to the account each month. In this case it is a good idea to set up a monthly standing order for the amount from your personal account to your business account. You can immediately take the money out if you want to.

You should certainly consider online and telephone banking. As an indication of what may be available the following is taken from a leaflet available from National Westminster Bank PLC.

Simple, straightforward business banking

The Foundation account offers a package with essential services to help you run your business smoothly. These include:

- **Business cheque book** – allowing you to pay for business-related purchases

- **Paying in book** – for paying in received cheques into your business account

- **Cashline Plus Card** – allowing you to make cashpoint withdrawals across the UK (and worldwide) and make SOLO payments

- **Standing Order and Direct Debits** – ideal for automatic payment of regular business bills such as electricity and phone

- **Statements** – clear, simple statements to keep you in the picture, with the option of e-statements if you register for digital banking

- **Digital and telephone banking** – do your banking when and where it suits you

- **Local branch network** – take advantage of our extensive local branch network to do your day to day banking transactions

- **Cost-effective business banking** – the Foundation Account is available on our Standard Tariff. Start-up free banking offers will also apply. Please refer to the charges leaflet for more details

Details of what is available from this bank may be obtained from www.natwest.com. As you would expect there are conditions in the small print and, of course, these terms may not be available at a later date. Check out what other banks offer too so you get the best deal to match your requirements.

Finally, people say some hard things about bankers. Nevertheless, many of them are helpful and nice, especially in local branches. So please smile at them and I'm sure they will be helpful.

Managing cashflow

Managing your cashflow is crucial. As explained elsewhere in this book it is possible and relatively common for a profitable business to be forced to close. The problem is not a shortage of profit, but an inability to pay the debts as they fall due. If you have ever been in the position of being unable to pay the salaries on time, you will understand why this matters.

The way to manage cashflow is firstly to have good information and then act on it, but good information comes first and it is vital. It comes mainly from three sources:

1. Your plan or budget. This is covered in detail in Chapter 5. It is important that it is kept up to date.

2. Your book-keeping system and accounts, which should also be kept up to date. This is covered in detail in Chapter 9.

3. The bank reconciliation which should be done frequently. This too is covered in detail in Chapter 9.

A revised cash forecast should be prepared from time to time, and when cash is expected to be tight it should be done frequently. It is likely that the two biggest factors will be money received from customers and money paid to suppliers. Money received from customers depends on your credit control which is covered next in this chapter.

There is an obvious incentive to pay the suppliers as slowly as possible. This could mean negotiating hard but fair terms that incorporate the longest possible payment period, then making payments at the limit of these agreed terms. If so, I heartily endorse the tactic. On the other hand it could mean disregarding the terms and cynically paying weeks or months late. As you may know to your cost, numerous businesses do adopt this approach. Many business people, and I have worked with some of them, believe that it is morally indefensible when their customers do it to them, but no more than common sense when they do it to their suppliers. You may have seen books that euphemistically endorse the practice. I believe that this is morally wrong and sometimes has unfortunate practical consequences.

Deliberately paying late is bound to annoy your suppliers. As a consequence they may be less co-operative and seek to take an advantage elsewhere, perhaps by raising prices or not going the extra mile with service and delivery dates. Of course, some things just cannot be paid late, salaries being a large and obvious example.

Some removal of cash can be said to be discretionary. The payment of dividends from a company and a salary to yourself come into this category, and so, if you are operating on a self-employed basis, do your 'drawings'. This observation is made with some humility because it is realised that you will have essential living expenses. If capital expenditure is planned, perhaps hire purchase or leasing should be considered. This spreads the payments over a period – probably a period of years.

In conclusion, cashflow planning should be realistic. Optimism has many advantages, but not in this area. If there is going to be a problem, the facts should be faced and remedial action planned.

Credit control

A good place to start is to ask yourself the question 'Should I allow credit?'. The answer is likely to be yes, but do consider the point. If you do not allow credit, you will save some time and probably some trouble. If you plan to run a shop or sell directly to the public, it might not be necessary. Having said that, what follows assumes that credit will be allowed.

Credit control is important for a lot of reasons, one of them being that it will have a major effect on your cash flow. Another is that poor credit control may be a factor in incurring bad debts. It is well known that late payments sometimes have a tendency to turn into non-payments.

Many people hate asking for payment and constantly find reasons for not doing so. This is completely the wrong attitude. Assuming that you have kept your side of the bargain, a late payer is cheating. You are absolutely right to press for payment according to the terms of the transaction. When you do this it is best to proceed according to the three Fs:

- Firm

- Fair

- Friendly

It is asking for trouble not to agree the payment terms at the outset and ideally these should be signed off by the buyer. The customer should be in no doubt what is expected and that he or she will be required to make payments on time. Invoices should be sent out very promptly and both invoices and statements should prominently show the payment terms.

It pays to get to know key people in your customer's organisation and this includes the person in the accounts office responsible for making payments. Of course this only applies if you are selling to companies of a significant size or equivalent businesses. You should request payment as soon as the money is due and not delay. Your telephone is probably the most effective way of doing this, but alternatives (or additional methods) include personal visits, e-mails and letters. In doing this remember the three Fs – Firm, Fair and Friendly.

If payment has not been received in a period that you are willing to tolerate, you should stop any further business and, of course, tell the customer why. You should also, almost always, issue a seven day warning letter and then proceed to legal action. This may be by using the services of a solicitor or other credit specialist, or by doing it yourself. It is not nearly as difficult as is often supposed. If there is a reasonable dispute (as opposed to an unreasonable one) you should of course try hard to resolve it before issuing the seven day warning letter and certainly before actually taking legal action. So long as the customer can find the money to pay, and they usually can even if they say otherwise, this is very likely to get you the money. It is likely to lose you a customer, but you probably do not want this particular one anyway.

All the above has general application, but the following additional points may be helpful for some businesses:

4. It may be a good idea to have a set of detailed terms and conditions. These should be drawn up with legal advice and it would be a mistake to try and do it yourself. They can cover all sorts of things including, if applicable, retention of title. You should be aware that just printing your terms of the back of order acknowledgements, invoices and statements does not make them legally effective. This should certainly be done, but what matters legally is the agreement at the time that the contract is made. The terms should be agreed (preferably signed) or at least last on the table at this point.

5. If you will be making significant purchases in connection with your work for a client or if the work will extend over a long period of

time, it may be sensible to ask for a deposit, stage payments or both.

6. It may be a good idea to ask for references on some prospective customers and take them up. Apart from anything else it is an early indication that you take credit control seriously.

Our personal experiences

Computers are not my strong point, but Dorothy is very proficient and uses hers a lot in her business. She follows the advice given in this chapter. She has a desktop computer and a laptop, and uses them extensively. She tried using cheap cartridges for her printer but found that they caused intermittent difficulties, so she reluctantly uses exclusively the manufacturer's brand.

Dorothy uses a local computer expert to help with problems from time to time. He is invaluable because she sometimes has to produce material to a tight timescale. It was she that suggested I should include the advice about knowing such a person.

We both like to give a good service and Dorothy has a great many letters, cards and e-mails thanking her for what she has done. I get a few complaints, quite often unjustified in my opinion. I do take them seriously and say sorry if I am wrong.

Our time management is probably unorthodox but it works well for us. We both keep our offices tidy and we follow the advice 'Don't put it down, put it away'. I frequently make rough lists as suggested in this chapter and it helps me a lot. I also follow the advice in the chapter to 'work with the grain'. I try to do undemanding things when I am feeling low or tired (or both as they tend to go together) and creative or demanding things when the mood is right, even if it is five o'clock in the morning. Fortunately the mood is usually right often enough to get the job done.

As I operate through a limited company I am obliged to have a separate bank account in the company's name. I originally had it at the bank and branch where I had my personal account and I took advantage of the bank's offer of free banking for new businesses. This ended after 18 months and at this point I transferred my account to another bank. This gives free banking provided that I deposit at least £1,000 every month. I have a monthly standing order of £1,000 from my personal account at the other bank. This is in case there is a month when I do not deposit the required minimum amount. It all seems a bit silly but it works. I also follow the rest of the banking advice and in particular I fend off their repeated attempts to sell me services that I do not need or want. At one point I got so fed up with the same approach being made over and over again that I asked the staff if they had ever seen the film 'Groundhog Day'.

Neither Dorothy nor I have problems managing cashflow, and fortunately neither of us have problems with credit control. We both have a relatively small number of customers, all of whom are prompt payers. So this is a thank you to Dorothy's customers and my seminar companies and publishers. I hope that you are as fortunate in this area.

Chapter 9

Book-keeping and accounts

There are two very good reasons why you should keep book-keeping records that conform with at least adequate minimum standards. The first is that it is a legal requirement that this be done in sufficient detail and with sufficient accuracy to support proper tax returns to HMRC. Furthermore, if your business is a limited company or a limited liability partnership, you are required by law to deliver statutory accounts to Companies House, from where they may be obtained by the public. These statutory accounts are of course prepared from the book-keeping records. The second reason is that, regardless of the legal requirements, good records will give you information that you need to run the business effectively.

You probably have three options:

1. You could pay someone to do everything for you. You would periodically give the chosen person armfuls of paper and let them get on with it. The book-keeper or accountant would keep the records up to date and, if able to do so, would prepare the accounts. The advantages are that, providing that you choose wisely, the book-keeper would probably do a good job and, whether you choose wisely or not, your time would be freed to run the business and earn revenue. Another advantage is that you would avoid doing a job that you might not enjoy. Disadvantages are the cost and the

fact that you would be separated from the figures and might lose touch with them. Periodic reviews by you of the figures would be important.

2. You could keep manual book-keeping records yourself. Perhaps you are willing and able to do everything yourself, including (if applicable) VAT returns and payroll calculations, as well as annual accounts if required. If not, you might keep the basic records up to date yourself and pay someone to do the specialised bits. This approach has a lot to commend it.

3. You could do everything described in Point 2 using a computer. (Sage's website is www.sage.co.uk). Sage sells a range of products but it is by no means the only company in the market. Alternatively you could simply use a spreadsheet such as Microsoft Excel. Arithmetical errors should be eliminated by a good software package or a well-structured spreadsheet. A common feature of manual book-keeping is that control accounts may not balance – for example, the total of individual debtors does not equal the sales ledger control account, or the VAT control account does not match the VAT return. This should not happen with computerised book-keeping. Bank reconciliations should be quicker and easier on a computer.

You may well be planning to do your accounts on a computer, but if you do not have much or any experience in accounting it will still be worth understanding the principles of manual book-keeping. This is because it will make it much easier for you to understand what the computer is doing. For example, if you are selling goods when you print out an invoice the computer will probably automatically debit the customer's account, add the value of the invoice to your sales and deduct the goods sold from stock. It will probably be easier to understand what the computer is doing if you think in terms of how you would do these processes manually.

This chapter explains the basic manual book-keeping records that are necessary and adequate in most small businesses. The information and layouts can readily be applied to computerised records. A prepurchased software package may not follow this exactly, but it will use the same principles. The chapter ends with some information about the accounts. This should be helpful, though you may well use a professional for this. The subjects covered are:

- Hints for your book-keeping system

- The end result

- Cash book

- Petty cash book

- Sales day book and sales ledger

- Purchase day book and purchase ledger

- Relationship with your own money

- VAT and payroll

- Bank reconciliation

- Accounts

- Our personal experiences

Hints for your book-keeping system

I was going to call this section of the chapter 'Hints for happy book-keeping' but then, even though I hope you enjoy keeping your financial records, I realised that this might not be appreciated. The following ideas should hopefully be helpful:

It is possible and perhaps likely that you will see book-keeping as a chore that takes up your time and gets in the way of running the business and earning money. It is nevertheless important and should not be neglected. Get the systems correct at the beginning, then there is much to be said for operating a policy of 'little and often'. It will seem much less daunting if you keep on top of it and frequently give it just a few minutes.

Do look at the figures and use the information to run the business and make decisions. The records should help a lot.

It is a good idea to make the categories of income and expense the same as the categories of income and expense that you have used in the business plan, and which you will probably use in future plans and budgets. This will help you monitor how you are doing through the year.

A good multi-column analysis book for manual records will probably cost about £35 and it will probably be big enough to last for several years. To cut down the expense it is a good idea to have different records at the front and back, rather than use two separate books. You could even have a third category in the middle of the book.

You should devise a numbering system for the invoices that you pay and for other vouchers, and enter the numbers in the books. This is so that you can easily cross-reference a book entry to the supporting voucher. This system can be as simple as starting at 1 and, if you have say 50 vouchers a month, arriving at 6,000 ten years later. These vouchers should be retained, perhaps in box files. They should be kept available for a possible HMRC check for up to six years.

It is likely that you will use an accountant or other professional to prepare your accounts based on the book-keeping records that you will maintain. It is sensible to discuss your book-keeping systems with this person before you set them up. This should ensure that you provide what is wanted for this purpose.

The end result

If your accountant prepares the accounts from a proper double entry set of records, most of the entries to these records (which may well be called the nominal ledger) will be made from the so-called books of prime entry. Various entries will be made in the books of prime entry, which will have suitable analysis columns, and periodically (perhaps monthly or quarterly) the totals of the columns will be transferred to the nominal ledger.

You may well have outside help to maintain the nominal ledger and produce the accounts, with you just writing up the books of prime entry. For this reason this chapter concentrates on the books of prime entry, which are:

• Cash book

• Petty cash book

• Sales day book

- Purchase day book

Cash book

What is cash? The narrowest definition is coins and bank notes, but much more realistically it includes cheques and other receipts and payments going into and out of the business's bank account. The cash book records and analyses all these receipts and payments. Some cash books cover both bank entries and cash entries, but it can all get rather complicated. Other businesses have a cash book for bank entries and a petty cash book for cash entries. This chapter follows the principle of two books and the cash book described here is just for bank entries.

The following is an extremely simple example of a cash book.

RECEIPTS							PAYMENTS	
Date		Folio	Amount £	Date			Folio	Amount £
1 Sept	Balance	b/d	800.00	1 Sept	4001	Arkwright	PL3	29.16
4 Sept	Cross and Co	SL6	101.10	2 Sept	4002	Business rates	NL4	290.00
9 Sept	Figg Ltd	SL12	17.11	6 Sept	4003	Stevens Ltd	PL7	34.12
13 Sept	Morgan Ltd	SL17	34.19	9 Sept	4004	Wilson Bros	PL19	47.11
18 Sept	Peters and Brown	SL3	700.00	12 Sept	4005	Crabbe and Co	PL8	39.12
30 Sept	Trapp Ltd	SL22	1,091.00	17 Sept	4006	Carter	PL2	200.00
				19 Sept	4007	Jenkins	PL12	56.99
				23 Sept	4008	Champion and Co	PL17	450.00
				24 Sept	4009	Stationery	NL8	290.00
				29 Sept	4010	Barton and Hicks	PL1	300.00
				30 Sept	Balance		c/d	1,006.90
			2,743.40					2,743.40
1 Oct	Balance	b/d	1,006.90					

Please note the following features:

4. There is a receipts side and a payments side. The rules of book-keeping require the receipts to go on the left. It is a short, simple example and there would probably be more entries in practice.

5. The cash book is one of the books of prime entry and the totals will be transferred to the main ledger, often known as the nominal ledger. Folio details identify the accounts where the entries are posted. You can devise your own system but, for example, PL3 means that Arkwright is account number 3 in the purchase ledger.

6. The cash book is for direct receipts and payments. Sales and purchases on credit should go into the sales ledger and purchase ledger respectively.

7. The cash book should be ruled off and balanced from time to time, and this is often done monthly. In the example there was £800.00 in the bank on 31st August and this was brought down on the receipts side on 1st September. If there had been an overdraft, the figure would have been brought down on the other side. At the end of the month the figure to make it balance is put in and the two columns are added. At the end of September there was £1,006.90 in the bank and this was carried down into October.

8. The example records the receipts and payments which is a good start, but there is no analysis of the figures. Analysis will in practice almost certainly be needed and the following shows how just the payments side might look. You will notice that a VAT column is included.

Date			Folio	Total	VAT	Purchase Ledger	Business Rates	Stationery
				£	£	£	£	£
1 Sept	4001	Arkwright	PL3	29.16		29.16		
2 Sept	4002	Business rates	NL4	290.00			290.00	
6 Sept	4003	Stevens Ltd	PL7	34.12		34.12		
9 Sept	4004	Wilson Bros	PL19	47.11		47.11		
12 Sept	4005	Crabbe and Co	PL8	39.12		39.12		
17 Sept	4006	Carter	PL2	200.00		200.00		
19 Sept	4007	Jenkins	PL12	56.99		56.99		
23 Sept	4008	Champion and Co	PL17	450.00		450.00		
24 Sept	4009	Stationery	NL8	290.00	48.34			241.66
29 Sept	4010	Barton and Hicks	PL1	300.00		300.00		
30 Sept	Balance		c/d	1,736.50	48.34	1,156.50	290.00	241.66
				1,006.90				
				£2,743.40				

PAYMENTS

Petty Cash Book

Cash payments may be included in the main cash book which was described in the last section of this chapter. Alternatively they may be recorded in a separate petty cash book. Petty cash is used for the payment of notes and coins. The word 'petty' means small or trivial and usually only small sums of cash are involved. The principles of the petty cash book are the same as the principles of the cash book. The following is an extremely simple example of a petty cash book.

Date	Details of expense	Voucher no.	Total	VAT	Stamps	Petrol
			£	£	£	£
2 May	Stamps	1	10.00		10.00	
16 May	Petrol	2	18.48	3.08		15.40
29 May	Stamps	3	10.00		10.00	
			38.48	3.08	20.00	15.40
31 May	Balance c/d		11.52			
			50.00			

148 WORKING FOR YOURSELF

This example operates with a float of £50.00 using the imprest system. £38.48 will be put into the petty cash at the end of May to restore the float to this amount.

Sales day book and sales ledger

The sales day book lists invoices to your customers. The following is a typical example, though the design can vary according to individual preference and business circumstances.

Date	Customer	Invoice no	Folio no	Goods total	VAT	Invoice total
				£	£	£
1 June	Bigg and Son	1001	B4	100.00	20.00	120.00
4 June	Carter Ltd	1002	C1	200.00	40.00	240.00
12 June	XYZ Ltd	1003	X1	50.00	10.00	60.00
17 June	Martin Bros	1004	M2	100.00	20.00	120.00
26 June	Fishers Ltd	1005	F5	10.00	2.00	12.00
30 June	Dawson Ltd	1006	D2	20.00	4.00	24.00
				480.00	96.00	576.00

Please note the following about each column:

- **Date**: This is the date of each individual invoice.

- **Customer**: This is the customer to which each individual invoice is addressed

- **Invoice no**: Each invoice must be individually numbered

- **Folio no**: This is the identifying code to each individual sales ledger account

- **Goods total**: This is the total value of each invoice excluding VAT. Sometimes this is further divided to include different totals for different product groups. The example given only shows total sales. £480.00 will be credited to the profit and loss account

- **VAT**: This is the VAT charged on each individual invoice
- **Invoice total**: This is the total amount of each individual invoice and the amount that the customer has to pay.

Had there been any credit notes issued they would have been entered as bracketed figures, and they would have reduced the totals.

If you only have one customer, you will not need a sales ledger. Nor will you need a sales ledger if your sales are entirely for cash. On the other hand, businesses that sell on credit may have many customers. For them, an efficient sales ledger is essential.

A sales ledger account is divided in the middle with debit on the left and credit on the right. There will be one account for each customer and the postings to it are:

- **Debit** - invoices issued
- **Credit** - credit notes issued
- **Credit** - cash received
- **Credit** - invoices written off as bad debts

Normally the debits on each account will exceed the credits. This means that the account has a debit balance which is the amount owed to the business by the customers.

Purchase day book and purchase ledger

If you have understood the sales day book and sales ledger you will have no problem with the purchase day book and the purchase ledger. This is because they are mirror images and operate in exactly the same way, though the purchase day book and purchase ledger apply to goods and services that you buy, rather than to goods and services that you sell. Of course if you do not buy on credit all your purchases can go through the cash book and you will not need a purchase day book or a purchase ledger.

The purchase day book is the medium through which a batch of suppliers' invoices is posted into the nominal ledger and into the purchase ledger. A typical purchase day book looks as follows.

Date	Customer	Invoice no	Folio no	Goods total	VAT	Invoice total
				£	£	£
1 July	Jones Ltd	3001	J8	100.00	20.00	120.00
9 July	King and Co	3002	K3	300.00	60.00	360.00
13 July	ABC Ltd	3003	A1	50.00	10.00	60.00
20 July	Dodd & Carr	3004	D2	200.00	40.00	240.00
28 July	Sugar Co Ltd	3005	S8	30.00	6.00	36.00
				680.00	136.00	816.00

It is periodically ruled off and totalled, perhaps monthly or quarterly.

The layout of the purchase ledger is similar to the layout of the sales ledger. Postings to it are:

- **Credit** - suppliers' invoices received

- **Debit** - suppliers' credit notes received

- **Debit** - cash payments made

Each purchase ledger account will normally have a credit balance and this represents the amount owing to the supplier by the business.

Relationship with your own money

You should separate your own money from the book-keeping records of your business. This is essential if you operate as a limited company and very desirable if you operate as a sole trader.

A limited company is a distinct legal entity that is separate from the person or persons who own shares in it. As a director you may have an account with it, and at any given time it may owe money to you or you may owe money to it. Payments to and from you should go through the cash book. If you are a sole trader, it will very probably have a bank account separate from your own and just for the business. Payments to and from you should go through the cash book. All this might be hard to understand and go against your instincts, but it is the right way to do it. It is likely that the balance sheet of your business will show money owing to or from you.

VAT and payroll

If your business will be registered for VAT, your book-keeping records must capture the VAT element of the sales that you make and the VAT element of the purchases that you make. This is done by putting a VAT column as part of the analysis in the books of prime entry. This has been done in the examples shown in this chapter. When all the columns have been totalled the figures will be used to compile the VAT return.

If you will employ anyone, you must keep adequate payroll records. Remember that if your business is conducted as a limited company, you will be an employee and perhaps the only employee. The money that you pay yourself as a salary or bonus (though not as dividends) must be put through the payroll records, and PAYE and national insurance must be deducted. This is not the case if you operate as a sole trader. Payroll records are kept separately from the book-keeping records. The net payments to employees must be entered in the cash book, and so must payments to HMRC for tax deducted and national insurance.

Bank reconciliation

The balance in the cash book should regularly be reconciled with the balance on the bank statement, and it will often be found that the figures are not the same. The writer Ernest Hemingway often did not bother to bank cheques that he received, preferring instead to use them as bookmarks. After his death his house was found to contain many unbanked cheques, some as much as 20 years old. Although the cheques were very seriously out of date many of them were subsequently honoured. This is an extreme example of why the bank statement balance might not be the same as the cash book balance and why it is necessary to reconcile the two figures. Such bizarre behaviour is unlikely in businesses, but bank reconciliations are necessary to show that mistakes have not been made (if this is the case), to identify any errors so that they can be corrected and to properly control the cash resources and borrowing.

Possible reasons for differences in the two figures to be reconciled are:

- Cheques written in the cash book have not yet been debited to the bank statement.

- Receipts written in the cash book have not yet been credited to the bank statement.

- Items have been debited to the bank statement that have not yet been written in the cash book. Common examples are direct debits, standing orders and bank charges.

- Receipts have been credited to the bank statement that have not yet been written in the cash book. This could, for example, include a receipt from a customer paid directly to the bank account by the BACS system.

- You have made a mistake. Perhaps the wrong amount has been written into the cash book or a paying-in slip has been added incorrectly.

- Customers have made electronic transfers into your bank account of which you are unaware.

An extremely simple bank reconciliation, based on the cash book shown earlier in this chapter might look as follows.

Balance per cash book at 30th September		1,006.90
Add cheques not yet presented:		
4008	450.00	
4009	290.00	
4010	300.00	
		1,040.00
		2,046.90
Less receipt not yet on statement		1,091.00
Balance per bank statement at 30th September		955.90

Accounts

One of the purposes of book-keeping records is to enable accounts to be prepared. Statutory accounts prepared in certain ways are compulsory for a limited company, and these must be sent to all shareholders, Companies House and HMRC. There is more freedom about the accounts of a sole trader, but they will be needed for tax purposes and by the owner of the business. If there is bank borrowing by either a limited company or a sole trader, it is likely that they will be of great interest to the bank.

It is likely, though not of course certain, that someone else will prepare your accounts, especially if you operate by means of a limited company. You might choose to skip this section of the chapter, but it might be useful to see an extremely simple example of how accounts are prepared. The following is for a service company, as stock and the sale of goods makes things more complicated. Tax is ignored, which is rather a big thing to ignore, and the accounts are for internal use and not in a form suitable for publication.

The totals in the books of prime entry are posted to the nominal ledger, and the accountant will probably make a few adjustments and additional postings. A trial balance will then be listed and the total of the debit balances must equal the total of the credit balances. If they do not do so, a mistake has been made. The debits in the trial balance are either expenses in the profit and loss account or assets in the balance sheet. The credits in the trial balance are either income in the profit and loss account or liabilities in the balance sheet. This may be confusing but it is consistent with the principles adopted by the founding father of double entry book-keeping. This was a Franciscan monk called Luca Pacioli who recorded them in 1493.

Mercial Consultants

Trial Balance

	£	£
Bank	7,416	
Computer equipment	2,000	
Miscellaneous expenses	3,219	
Motor vehicle	6,000	
Office costs	17,112	
Sales		49,400
Trade creditors		7,862
Trade debtors	6,219	
Travel	15,296	
	57,262	57,262

Mercial Consultants

Profit and Loss Account

	£	£
Sales		49,400
Less Expenses:		
Office costs	17,112	
Travel	15,296	
Miscellaneous expenses	3,219	
		35,627
Net profit		13,773

Mercial Consultants

Balance Sheet

	£	£
Fixed assets		
Motor vehicle	6,000	
Computer equipment	2,000	
		8,000
Current assets		
Trade debtors	6,219	
Bank	7,416	
	13,635	
Less current liabilities		
Trade creditors	7,862	
		5,773
		13,773
Reserves		13,773

Our personal experiences

I am an accountant so it would be surprising if I did not do the book-keeping and accounts for my company as described in this chapter. I do the book-keeping and accounts for my wife's business on the same principles as well. I quite enjoy book-keeping, which some people would say makes me a rather sad person.

Chapter 10
Dealing with Tax

Benjamin Franklin wrote 'But in this world nothing can be said to be certain, except death and taxes'. He was surely right because he was a great man who achieved great things. His many accomplishments included the invention of the lightning conductor, which he tested by flying a kite in a thunderstorm. It is fitting therefore that we conclude with this chapter on tax. There are rewards and peace of mind in getting it right. The rates, allowances and thresholds are adjusted each year. Those quoted in this chapter are for the tax year ending on 5th April 2013.

Tax is inherently complicated and, even though I have tried to make the chapter as straightforward as possible, it may need a lot of concentration. This may be a good reason, for a fee of course, for employing the services of an accountant. He or she should be able to save you work, explain things to you and suggest legitimate ways of paying less tax. A reputable accountant will, like me, only suggest legal and legitimate ways of saving tax, which is of course exactly what you want.

The advice in this chapter is inevitably very simplified and should be treated as a guide only. There are other things that may affect your obligations and the tax that you pay, which is a reason for using the services of an accountant.

It may well not happen, but you could have to show your records to HMRC and justify what you have done. This is an excellent reason for keeping your book-keeping records in good order and keeping invoices, receipts etc. You should invent a simple system for numbering them so that they can easily be located and cross-referenced.

It is possible that you might enjoy paying a lot of tax, but it is likely that you would like to arrange your affairs so that you pay the minimum that can legitimately be arranged. I stress the word 'legitimately' because this book will not encourage you to illegitimately evade tax. Having made this clear, you may be encouraged by the words of Lord Clyde delivered during his judgment in the case of Ayrshire Pullman Motor Services v Inland Revenue 1929. He said:

> 'No man in the country is under the smallest obligation, moral or other, so to arrange his legal relations to his business or property as to enable the Inland Revenue to put the largest possible shovel in his stores. The Inland Revenue is not slow, and quite rightly, to take every advantage which is open to it under the Taxing Statutes for the purpose of depleting the taxpayer's pocket. And the taxpayer is in like manner entitled to be astute to prevent, so far as he honestly can, the depletion of his means by the Inland Revenue.'

If you are self-employed, you might consider employing your wife, husband or partner. If they have little or no other income, you can utilise their personal allowance. Even if they do have other income, it might stop you having to pay higher rate tax. HMRC will not like it if he or she is paid more than can be justified by the work that they do. Paying someone £30,000 a year for typing a few letters is asking for trouble, but it might not be hard to justify a moderate and reasonable figure.

If you have a limited company, you may find that it is advantageous to take money out by means of dividends rather than a salary. It is, though, probably a good idea to pay yourself a salary slightly in excess of the personal allowance. This is to preserve some national insurance benefits.

If you have been in full-time employment before starting on your own and particularly if the change is made well into the tax year, it is worth sending your P45 to the tax office. You may be able to get a refund of some or all of the tax deducted by your employer. It will not make any difference in the long run, but it could be a welcome early boost to your cashflow.

The topics covered in this chapter are:

- The requirement to register with HMRC
- The taxes that must be paid
- National insurance
- Your self-assessment tax form
- Payment dates for tax due
- The need to have money available
- Expenses that can legitimately be set against income for tax purposes
- Value added tax
- Our personal experiences

The requirement to register with HMRC

It is a legal requirement that a new business be notified to HMRC within three months of it starting to trade. The penalty for not doing so is £100 and the penalties for continued and more serious failure are greater.

If you are operating as a sole trader or part of a general partnership, this can be done online at www.hmrc.gov.uk. Alternatively it can be done by calling the helpline for the newly self-employed which is 08459 154515, or by completing form CWF1 which may be obtained from a local HMRC office. Information for the newly self-employed is available online at http://www.hmrc.gov.uk/selfemployed

If you are operating through the medium of a limited company or a limited liability partnership you must complete form CT41G. This will normally be sent to the registered office by HMRC, which will have been informed of the new company or LLP by Companies House. Alternatively (or if it is not received) the form may be downloaded from www.hmrc.gov.uk or obtained from a local HMRC office.

The taxes that must be paid

If you are self-employed as a sole trader or partner, you must pay income tax on the profits.

A registered company is a separate legal entity which must pay corporation tax on its profits. Assuming that profits are made and that the money is available, some or all of them may be extracted from the company. You will have a lot of freedom about the timing of this which is an advantage for tax planning purposes. Your salary or bonus is subject to PAYE which must be deducted by the company and paid monthly to HMRC. Your dividends (if any) must be declared on your self-assessment form. Dividends are paid out of after tax profits and there is no further tax to pay unless you are a higher rate tax payer.

Current tax rates (including national insurance) can be obtained from: www.hmrc.gov.uk/rates.

National insurance

National insurance is technically not a tax, though it is exceedingly difficult to tell the difference. Governments have not been above raising national insurance rather than income tax in order to fulfil a promise not to raise tax.

A self-employed person is liable to pay both Class 2 and Class 4 National Insurance Contributions. Class 2 is £2.65 per week unless his or her earnings are less than £5,595 (2012-13 limit) and he or she has applied for a Certificate of Exemption. Class 2 NICs are payable monthly or quarterly. Class 4 is payable by self-employed persons according to the level of their profits as determined for income tax purposes. For 2012-13 Class 4 NIC is levied at the rate of 9% of trading profits between £7,605 and £42,475. Earnings in excess of the upper profits limit attract Class 4 NIC at the rate of 2%.

If you operate through the medium of a registered company or LLP, Class 1 NIC is payable on your salary and bonuses. Secondary contributions are payable by the company or LLP. These are generally known as employees and employers' national insurance contributions. Employee's NIC will be deducted at source and paid over monthly with the employer's contribution. National insurance contributions do not apply to dividends.

Your self-assessment form

You may not have previously completed a self-assessment tax form, but if you are self-employed, are a director, receive dividends or are liable to higher rate tax it is likely to be a requirement. HMRC will almost certainly send a form to you, but if it does not do so you should request one. It is your responsibility to get the form and supply the correct information. Of course submission may be done online which is encouraged by HMRC.

Income tax is based on a tax year running from 6th April to 5th April in the following year. If the form is submitted on paper, it must arrive by the following 31st October (just under seven months from the end of the tax year). If it is submitted online, it must be done by the following 31st January (just under ten months from the end of the tax year). If submission is made on paper by 31st October, HMRC will calculate the amount of tax due. If submission is later than 31st October, HMRC will not do this and you must do the calculation yourself. If submission is made online, HMRC will calculate the tax due.

Payment dates for tax due

As a self-employed person your chosen accounting period can finish on any date that you choose and does not have to be the same as the tax year which ends on 5th April. HMRC accepts an accounting year ending on 31st March as equivalent to one ending on 5th April and in practice there are certain advantages in picking this date. The payment dates for the income tax (including Class 4 National Insurance Contributions) on profits is best illustrated with an example.

Gavin starts self-employment on 1st April 2012 and completes his first accounts for the year to 31st March 2013. He submits his self-assessment tax form online as required by 31st January 2014. His payment dates are as follows:

- 31st January 2014 Tax on profit for year to 31st March 2013 plus 50% of tax on estimated profit for year to 31st March 2014

- 31st July 2014 Second 50% of tax on estimated profit for year to 31st March 2014

HMRC will estimate the tax based on the actual profit for the previous period. If (as is inevitable) the estimate is too high or too low, the tax payment is adjusted up or down at the next payment. If you feel that the estimate is too high you can have it reduced to a lower figure. However, interest must be paid if the tax payable turns out to be higher than this estimate.

The pattern of six monthly payments on 31st January and 31st July will continue for subsequent years.

Companies must pay corporation tax nine months and one day from the end of the accounting period. This is on the actual profits for the period and there is no payment based on estimates. Large companies must pay by instalments but this will not affect you. So, for example, corporation tax on profits for the year to 31st March 2013 is due on 1st January 2014.

The need to have money available

The self-employed pay tax and most national insurance in arrears, unlike an employed person who has them deducted at source under the PAYE system. For a person starting a new business the first payment is due 22 months after the start of the business. The delay becomes smaller but payment is still made significantly in arrears. This is a big advantage and may be a factor in choosing self-employment, though of course when self-employment finishes tax must subsequently be paid to catch up.

It is all to easy to not fully take the tax payment dates into account and not have the money readily available when payment is due. This can have serious consequences including penalties and interest, but also on the family budget. The amounts and looming payment dates should on no account be forgotten. The mills of the Revenue grind slowly but they grind exceedingly small. Some people save a fixed monthly sum into a separate account or put aside a certain percentage of sales made.

Expenses that can legitimately be set against income for tax purposes

The basic test for a company is expenditure that is incurred "wholly, exclusively and necessarily" for the purposes of the business. The basic test for a self-employed person is expenditure that is incurred "wholly and exclusively" for the purposes of the business. The test for a self employed person is not quite so rigorous, though in practice it will probably make little or no difference.

Not all expenses are allowable. For example, most entertaining and hospitality is not allowable and if it has been charged in the Profit and Loss Account it must be added back for the purpose of the tax calculation. There are special rules for capital expenditure which goes into the Balance Sheet rather than the Profit and Loss Account. Depreciation in the Profit and Loss Account must be added back and capital allowances substituted. These write down the value of fixed assets according to the tax rules. However, if you have prepared a proper set of accounts, it is probable that most of the expenses in the Profit and Loss Account are allowable for tax purposes.

You may be disappointed but probably not surprised to know that if you work from home, not all household expenses can be set against tax. However, a fair and reasonable proportion of them can. For example, if your house has six rooms (plus bathroom, kitchen, hall etc) and if one of the rooms is used exclusively for business, it is probably fair and reasonable to charge to the business one sixth of such things as gas, electricity, water, council tax etc. This does not extend to things such as gardening and painting the house.

If you have a separate telephone exclusively for business, the total cost including rental can be charged to the business. If you use a family telephone for business calls, the total bills should be apportioned in a fair way, perhaps 50/50. The same applies to mobile phones.

If a motor vehicle is used exclusively for business purposes, total running costs are allowable. If, as is probably more likely, a motor vehicle is only partly used for business purposes, complicated rules apply. However, an alternative which is likely to be attractive is the mileage allowance. For the tax year 2012/13 this is 45 pence for the first 10,000 business miles and 25 pence for subsequent business miles. Such things as tolls and parking can also be charged. A record of business journeys should be kept as the mileage claimed may possibly one day have to be justified to HMRC.

Value added tax

Registration is compulsory when a business makes taxable supplies over a predetermined limit. The limit is based on annual gross turnover and for the tax year 2012-13 it is £77,000. Registration is required where one of two conditions is satisfied:

1. When, at the end of any month, the gross taxable turnover during the previous 12 months, on a rolling basis, exceeds £77,000.

2. When there are reasonable grounds for believing that the value of taxable supplies to be made within the following 30 days will exceed £77,000.

It is possible to register voluntarily even though taxable supplies will be less than the £77,000 limit. Whether or not this is a good idea depends on individual circumstances and an individual choice. A disadvantage of registering is the time and bureaucracy involved in registering, keeping the necessary records and making regular VAT returns and payments. Registration is achieved using the website www.hmrc.gov.uk.

A consequence of registration is that you must charge VAT on your sales and may recover the VAT that you pay on business expenses. Assuming that the former are greater than the latter, the difference must be paid to HMRC. If you do not register, you do not charge VAT on your sales and you cannot recover the VAT element of your business expenses. The VAT element of your business expenses reduces your profit, but this does consequently reduce the income tax or corporation tax payment.

It is probably worth registering if you sell primarily or exclusively to VAT-registered businesses. Your customers will not mind because they will be able to recover the VAT that you have charged them. You will be able to recover the VAT that you have paid on business expenses. Consider this scenario:

- Sales = £50,000

- VAT charged (20% x £50,000) = £10,000

- VAT element of expenses paid = £3,000

In the course of a year you would pay £7,000 (£10,000 less £3,000) to HMRC. Your profit, which is subject to income tax or corporation tax, would be increased by £3,000.

It is probably a mistake to register if you sell primarily or exclusively to the public or businesses that are not registered for VAT. This is because your customers cannot recover the VAT that you charge and this makes your prices to them 20% higher. If you do not register, you of course cannot recover the VAT element of the business expenses that you pay. An effective 20% price rise to your customers is a massive reason not to register. In fact some businesses take steps to keep their turnover just below the £77,000 threshold in order to avoid registration.

VAT registration, returns and payments are now done exclusively electronically. The paper alternative is no longer available. Most businesses submit quarterly VAT returns and payments. Outputs are the VAT charged in the quarter. Inputs are the VAT element of invoices from suppliers entered in the quarter. So long as outputs are greater than inputs, a payment to HMRC will be due and must be paid within a month and seven days of the end of the quarter. Outputs and inputs are based on invoices to customers issued and invoices from suppliers entered, regardless of whether or not payment has been made or received. If sales invoices are raised late in the quarter and if customers are slow to pay, VAT must be paid to HMRC before it has been received from customers. This may be a reason for raising invoices early in the quarter, though credit control considerations may say get the invoices out as soon as possible. A number of special VAT schemes may be available and three in particular are worth consideration:

Annual accounting

Businesses with an annual turnover not exceeding £1,350,000 (excluding VAT) may be authorised to use the annual accounting scheme. Nine monthly payments or three quarterly payments, in either case based on the previous year's VAT liability, are made by direct debit and a final balancing payment is made with the VAT return at the end of the second month following the allocated VAT year.

The advantage of annual accounting, which may be used in conjunction with the flat rate scheme, is that it saves time and work.

Cash accounting

This may be available, providing that certain conditions are met, for businesses having an annual turnover of not more than £1,350,000. The VAT return is geared, for both outputs and inputs, to the dates that money is received and VAT invoices are paid, rather than to the dates that sales invoices are issued and suppliers' invoices entered. This is attractive if customers pay slowly or erratically.

Flat-rate scheme for small businesses

This may save a lot of money and be worth serious consideration. It can be used in conjunction with annual accounting but not in conjunction with cash accounting. It can be used where taxable turnover in the next year is expected to be not more than £150,000 and total business income is expected to be not more than £187,500.

A business registered for the flat-rate scheme will not recover its inputs (VAT that it has paid out), but will account for a flat-rate percentage of its VAT-inclusive turnover. The flat-rate percentage will depend on the sector in which the business operates and may be obtained from the HMRC website. There are administrative savings but the main attraction is the possible money saving. The biggest savings are where inputs (VAT paid on purchases) are low and the flat-rate percentage is generous. There is no substitute for doing your own estimated calculations. Consider the following hypothetical scenario.

Annual sales excluding VAT	£50,000
VAT charged	£10,000
Annual sales including VAT	£60,000
VAT paid on purchases	£2,000
Flat rate percentage	12%

If the flat-rate scheme is not used, VAT of £8,000 (£10,000 less £2,000) must be paid to HMRC. If the flat-rate scheme is used, VAT of £7,200 (12% x £60,000) must be paid to HMRC, an annual saving of £800. This would be extra profit and as such would be subject to income tax or corporation tax.

Our personal experiences

I am an accountant and I personally do all the book-keeping and tax work for my company 'Roger Mason Limited'. I do the same for my wife in her self-employed role as a Civil Funeral Celebrant. It is not very demanding and I think that I do a good job, though as Mandy Rice-Davies said in a different context, 'He would say that, wouldn't he?'. I follow the philosophy of claiming everything that can legitimately be claimed, but nothing that can not legitimately be claimed.

My wife puts a sum of money away each month, the amount varying according to her level of business in the month. This is available to pay the tax when it becomes due. I do not do this, but I do ensure that I have the money available when the tax has to be paid.

My clients are all VAT-registered and it therefore made sense for Roger Mason Limited to register voluntarily. The company uses the flat-rate scheme and makes a significant saving as a consequence.